NE~~~~~~
HA~~~~~~

For

San Francisco

NEWCOMER'S ™
HANDBOOK
For
San Francisco

FIRST BOOKS

P.O. Box 578147
Chicago, IL 60657
773-276-5911
http://www.firstbooks.com

First Edition

Author: Michael Bower
Publisher and Editor: Jeremy Solomon
Associate Editor: Bernadette Duperron
Contributors: Alex Kline, Frank Slacik
Design: Art Machine
Map: Art Machine

ISBN: 0-912301-34-1

ISSN: 1089-9731

Manufactured in the United States of America.

Published by First Books, Inc., P.O. Box 578147, Chicago, IL 60657, 773-276-5911.

WELCOME to San Francisco, known by natives and long time residents as "The City." Many visitors have lost their hearts to this cosmopolitan collection of stunning urban and ocean vistas and returned to make it home. Perhaps you are one of them. Regardless of where you're leaving, chances are you're going to love it here.

San Francisco is relatively small when compared to places like New York City, Los Angeles or Chicago, only 48 square miles in fact. But what it has to offer, in terms of culture, fair weather, job opportunities, higher education and recreational options, far exceeds what might be expected from such a compact community.

Nowhere else in America can you ride a moving national landmark, San Francisco's cable cars, taking in some of the most beautiful scenery anywhere. Among the sites you'll be able to drink in at your leisure, the San Francisco Bay, Alcatraz Island, Golden Gate Bridge, Golden Gate Park and the city skyline itself. You'll have little difficulty seeing those sights, as San Francisco has some of the cleanest big-city air in the country. That's largely due to the proximity of the mighty Pacific Ocean and steady winds that swiftly move the smog away, leaving shimmering blue skies behind. Many would say Bay Area meteorologists have one of the easiest jobs around, as the weather forecast is consistently "low clouds and fog overnight, clearing by mid-morning, giving way to afternoon sunshine." The temperature rarely dips below 40 degrees fahrenheit or above 80, except during the Indian Summer months of late August and September, when it can get into the 90's. That's about it, except for when it rains, which throws just about everybody for a loop.

Long a hotbed of alternative lifestyles, from its rowdy Barbary Coast days in the 19th century, to the 1950's Beat Generation of North Beach and the "make love not war" hippie/drug culture of Haight Ashbury in the 1960's, that unconventional tradition lives on in many areas. The city is home to a large, politically-active gay and lesbian population residing largely in the Castro and Mission districts. At the other end of the spectrum are the towering temples of capitalism and Western economic power that make up the compact downtown Financial District. Home to some of the country's largest banks, San Francisco is also the site of the Pacific Stock Exchange, despite talk over the past few years of moving it elsewhere.

The nine county San Francisco Bay Area is also high-tech heaven to all manner of inventor, computer programmer, software and hardware designer, internet guru, communications technologist, and entrepreneur. Home of the internationally known Silicon Valley, where the personal computer culture was born at Apple, and continues to be fashioned at numerous other companies, people here work in everything from t-shirts, shorts and sandals to European suits and silk ties. The Bay Area has been in the forefront of the movement to "dress down" the American workplace (it's the home of Levi Strauss and The Gap clothing giants). Jeans and sport-shirts can now be seen in high-rise office buildings every day of the week ... they're not just for Fridays anymore.

More than six million people make their homes in the Bay Area, but only about three-quarters of a million in the city proper. That population almost doubles during weekdays, as hundreds of thousands of motorists take to the local freeways and bridges in order to get to work. Some of the nation's worst morning and evening commutes are here, despite the existence of the sleek, clean and usually-efficient Bay Area Rapid Transit, or BART, system. Where the BART trains don't go, more than two dozen other transit systems do. They include buses, trolleys, cable cars, commuter trains, shuttles and ferry boats.

San Francisco also has more restaurants per person than any other U.S. city, according to local tourism officials, offering every cuisine imaginable. That translates into some very stiff competition between the eateries, many of which fail every year. Don't worry if your favorite shuts down, though, because chances are something equally good will take over the space.

San Francisco runs the gamut when it comes to housing options. Small studios are available in many parts of the city, including the area immediately around the Financial District. There are high rise apartment complexes on Russian and Nob hills with bay views to die for, immaculately maintained Victorian flats and single-family homes in Noe Valley, the Castro, the Haight and Cole Valley, penthouse condominiums and lofts South of Market, Mediterranean-style apartments and houses in the singles-Mecca of the Marina, row upon row of pleasant, relatively affordable residences in the Sunset and Richmond districts, and the mansions of Sea Cliff, Pacific Heights and Presidio Heights. Many consider San Francisco to be a singles town, but you'll soon discover that there are many areas that welcome families with open arms.

Keep in mind that this city is consistently listed at or very near the top of the least affordable places to live in the United States, and that applies to mortgages as well as rents. Recent surveys put the median price for a Bay Area home at $250,000 – $275,000. Rents are also on the rise. One recent survey found that rents in San Francisco were up by more than 11% from the previous year.

This book is intended to be a launching pad for your adventure into the wild, concrete canyons of San Francisco's downtown, all the way out to the fog-shrouded serenity of "the Avenues" and everything in between. We'll also look at the surrounding areas, if living in the city is not for you. We'll glance at Oakland, Berkeley, San Jose, Marin County and more, all along hoping to make your transition into life as a Bay Area resident as efficient and enjoyable as possible.

SAN FRANCISCO has more than two dozen neighborhoods or districts, each of which can be clearly defined, despite the fact that some of them meld into one another at the edges. One of the dominant features of San Francisco life is fog. London is perhaps the only city more famous for its fog than San Francisco. Locals call it "Mother Nature's air conditioner" and it's especially welcome during the Indian Summer months of late August and September. For those six to eight weeks residents wake up in homes blanketed by a mist so thick it feels like drizzle. It usually burns away by noon, giving way to clear blue skies and temperatures into the 90's. Then, just when you can't take the heat anymore, the fog tumbles into the Bay Area from the Pacific Ocean to the west, cooling temperatures down to the 40s and 50s so you can sleep. There are some areas of the city which get less fog than others, such as the Mission, Potrero Hill, Noe Valley and the Castro, but you won't be able to avoid it entirely. After you've been here for a while, chances are you'll grow to love the fog, if you don't already.

There are areas of the city blessed by certain smells, namely fresh brewed, dark Italian and French roast coffee in North Beach, steamed crab and freshly baked sourdough in the Northpoint/Fisherman's Wharf section, morning bagels in the Richmond, the salty bite of the Pacific Ocean along the western edge of the Sunset, and the sometimes disturbing odor of cable car brakes heating up as you descend some of the city's steepest slopes on Russian Hill and Nob Hill.

Much of this city's charm and vitality can be pinned on its ethnic diversity. The earliest non-native settlers came from Russia, Italy, Ireland, Germany, China, Japan and the Philippines, all of them establishing their own neighborhoods at first, and then branching out. That intracity migration continues today, most notably the Chinatown population spreading out into formerly Italian-dominated North Beach. All of this makes the city a vibrant and a stimulating locale to call home.

The following neighborhood profiles include information on each area, focusing on the general characteristics of the neighborhood, as well as information on housing, weather, public transit, post office locations, emergency services, hospitals, public safety agencies, local attractions and restaurant suggestions.

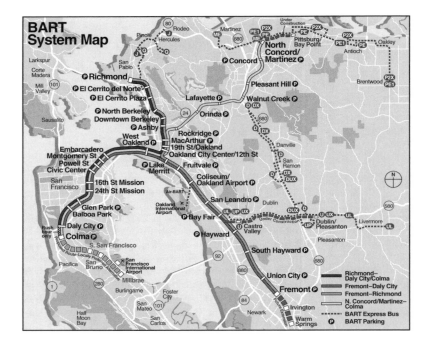

San Francisco

North Beach/Telegraph Hill

Russian Hill/Nob Hill

Pacific Heights/Marina/Cow Hollow

Richmond

Sunset/Parkside

Haight Ashbury

Stonestown/Park Merced/Ingleside

Glen Park/Diamond Heights

The Castro/Noe Valley

Mission/Bernal Heights

Potrero Hill

South of Market-SOMA

Excelsior/Crocker Amazon/Visitacion Valley

Surrounding Areas

North Bay

East Bay

Peninsula

South Bay

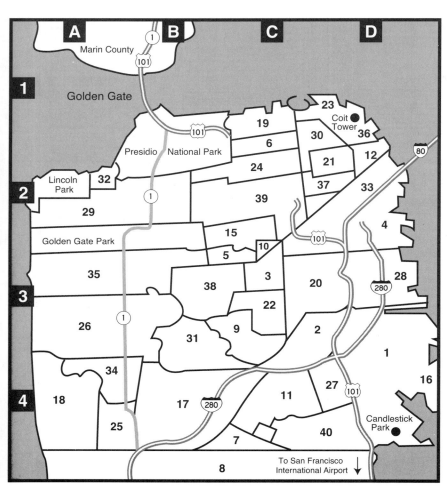

1. Bayview D-4	11. Excelsior C-4	21. Nob Hill C-2	31. St. Francis Wood B-3
2. Bernal Heights C-3	12. Financial District D-2	22. Noe Valley C-3	32. Seacliff A-2
3. Castro D-2	13. Forest Hill B-3	23. North Beach C-1	33. South of Market D-2
4. China Basin D-2	14. Glen Park C-4	24. Pacific Heights C-2	34. Stonestown A-1
5. Cole Valley B-3	15. Haight B-2	25. Park Merced A-4	35. Sunset A-3
6. Cow Hollow C-2	16. Hunter's Point D-4	26. Parkside A-3	36. Telegraph Hill D-1
7. Crocker Amazon B-4	17. Ingleside B-4	27. Portola C-4	37. Tenderloin C-2
8. Daly City B-4	18. Lake Merced A-4	28. Potrero Hill D-3	38. Upper Market B-3
9. Diamond Heights B-3	19. Marina C-1	29. Richmond A-2	39. Western Addition C-2
10. Dubole Triangle C-2	20. Mission C-3	30. Russian Hill C-1	40. Visitacion Valley C-4

NORTH BEACH/TELEGRAPH HILL

Boundaries: **East**, The Embarcadero; **West**, Columbus Avenue; **North**, Fisherman's Wharf; **South**; Broadway. (Telegraph Hill is in the northeast corner of North Beach.)

North Beach doesn't have a beach, but it used to, along the area's northern edge between Telegraph Hill on the east and Russian Hill on the west. It has since been covered with a series of piers and is now home to the tourist Mecca of Fisherman's Wharf.

Dozens of seafood restaurants can be found at the northern end of the Embarcadero, a beautifully remodeled thoroughfare that runs along the bayside edge of the city from the South of Market Area north. The Embarcadero terminates at the Fisherman's Wharf area that is just a short walk from the Cannery, Anchorage and Ghirardelli Square shopping centers. The latter is a former chocolate factory that still serves the dark confection in various forms, perhaps most notably, hot chocolate with real whipped cream, a body-warming treat on a chilly winter's morning as you wrap up your holiday shopping. Stroll along Fisherman's Wharf, take a look at the still-active fishing fleet moored here, nibble on a prawn cocktail "to go," and take in the rich smell of steaming crab and the equally rich sights of this bustling visitor's delight. Then pause for a moment, and savor the fact that you're no longer a tourist.

North Beach was once predominantly Italian, and it still retains much of that atmosphere, but it's now also home to a burgeoning Chinese-American population moving over from nearby Chinatown. As you might expect, North Beach has many Italian restaurants, from coffee and pastry joints, such as Cafe Trieste, where if the opera's not live it's being played in the juke box, to pizza parlors, such as North Beach Pizza and Tommaso's, to some of the finest upscale eateries in the city. Most notable is the Fior d'Italia overlooking Washington Square Park and The North Beach Restaurant, about a block away, on Stockton at Columbus. Other choices you can bank on for good, and often interesting food include, The Stinking Rose, which does just about everything that can be done to and with garlic, Mario's Bohemian Cigar Store, a local institution that makes what many locals will tell you is the best cappuccino in the city, and Rico's Mexican Restaurant, for some of the freshest, least expensive food around. There are scores of other good options for satisfying your hunger. These are just a few to whet your appetite.

North Beach is also the former home of the Beat Generation of 1950s poets, authors and critical thinkers, such as Lawrence Ferlinghetti, whose City Light's Bookstore still exists at its original location, Jack Kerouac, who's recently had a tiny local alleyway named in his honor, and Allen Ginsberg. Right across the alley from City Lights is Vesuvio, a still-active bar that played host to all three of them, and other beatniks of lesser renown. Another piece of San Francisco history is visible from City Lights, the world famous Condor Club, where topless pioneer Carol Doda bared near-all, sparking the Broadway topless scene. Since Carol moved on to other ventures the area has become a mere shadow of its former self. The Condor is now a trendy bistro, but it features dozens of artifacts from the Doda days, a history it proudly displays.

Most North Beach residents live in apartments, and vacancies are rare. After all, once you live here, why leave? It's a short walk to San Francisco's Financial District, and any kind of shopping you'd need to do. If you work downtown you probably will not need to own a car, as North Beach is served by buses and cable cars. Parking options are few, but if you do keep the car, you'll need to get a parking permit to park it on the hilly streets for more than two hours at a time. Also, remember to curb your wheels when you park on a hill. If the car is facing downhill, your front wheels must turn in towards the curb. If the car faces uphill, the front wheels should turn out from the curb. And, set that parking brake! Parking control officers will ticket you for not obeying the curbing rule. If your apartment doesn't come with a garage (most here don't) and you have the cash, check the newspaper's rental section and you may be able to find one.

Telegraph Hill is so named because it was the site of the West Coast's first telegraph station, from which spotters would look for ships entering San Francisco Bay through the Golden Gate. When a ship was sighted, spotters would notify port officials by Morse code of the impending arrival. The "Hill", as locals call the area, features breathtaking views of the bay, including Alcatraz Island, the former home of the notorious prison and convicts such as Al Capone and the "Birdman of Alcatraz" (who actually kept no birds while there), narrow streets lined with quaint cottages and picture-windowed condominiums, beautiful gardens and even fewer rental vacancies than the rest of North Beach. The most prominent feature of this area is Coit Tower, rising from the top of Telegraph Hill, a monument to the city's fire-fighters, funded by the private contribution of Lillie Hitchcock Coit. Check it out for the murals inside and the bay/city views outside.

Area Code: 415

Zip Code: 94133

Post Office: North Beach Station,1640 Stockton St., 956-3581.

Police Station: Central Station, 766 Vallejo Street, 553-1532; Community Police On Patrol, 362-4349.

Emergency Hospitals: California Pacific Medical Center, 2333 Buchanan, 923-3333; St. Francis Memorial Hospital, 900 Hyde St., 353-6000.

Library: 2000 Mason at Columbus, 274-0270.

Public Transportation: *MUNI buses* - 30 Stockton, 41 Union, 39 Coit, 32 Embarcadero, 42 Downtown Loop; *Cable Car* access to Hyde St. line at Ghirardelli Square area and Mason Street line at Bay and Taylor Streets. MUNI bus and Cable Car connections to BART and Light Rail stations along Market St.

RUSSIAN HILL/NOB HILL

Boundaries: *Russian Hill:* **East**, Columbus Ave.; **North**, Bay St.; **West**, Van Ness Ave.; **South**, Broadway. *Nob Hill:* **East**, Kearny St.; **North**, Broadway; **West**, Larkin St.; **South**, Sutter St.

Situated just west of North Beach, Russian Hill is a varied collection of high-rise condominiums, flats, apartments and single-family homes occupied by much of the city's elite. There's old and new money here, for which residents get some of the most spectacular views of the downtown skyline, San Francisco Bay, and Alcatraz.

Residents also get easy access to what's left of a once extensive cable car system, the brain-child of inventor Andrew Hallidie, who piloted the first cable car down Clay Street from Jones to Kearny and back in 1873. Word is Hallidie felt sorry for the horses that had to pull wagons up the hills. At its peak the system boasted 8 lines and more than 100 miles of track. Three lines remain today, two of which serve both Russian Hill and Nob Hill (Mason and Hyde), the third rumbles through Nob Hill and the Financial District along California Street.

One of San Francisco's all-time favorite tourist attractions is the section of Lombard Street referred to as the most crooked street in the world. The twisting street is situated on the eastern slope of Russian Hill. It's recently been reopened to traffic after an extensive refurbishment (tourists were pulling bricks out of the street and taking them home). Local residents, who pay a pretty penny for the honor of living here, are once again hearing the near-constant click of camera shutters and inhaling vehicle fumes as gleeful motorists navigate the eight near-hairpin turns in just one block. Russian Hill is dotted with dozens of tiny parks, many of which are reachable only by frighteningly steep stairs, not for the short of breath. But if you're up to the challenge, the views are worth the workout.

Apartments and flats are often available here, especially in the area including and immediately surrounding the northern end of Polk, Larkin and Hyde Streets. As in much of San Francisco, though, living here is not inexpensive, but, as in North Beach, persistence and patience may pay off. Once you've unpacked you can explore nearby Polk Gulch, the northern half of which is a trendy shopping zone packed with restaurants, movie theaters, boutiques, and a thriving coffee bar scene. The somewhat sleazy southern half contains good places to eat along with bars, liquor stores, leather shops, and adult entertainment outlets. Drugs and teen-runaways are still components of street life along this stretch of Polk.

Nob Hill, or "Snob Hill" as it's been derisively called, is situated directly south of Russian Hill, and is perhaps the most famous of San Francisco's hills (many speak of the city's seven hills, but there are actually 43 that come with names). Nob Hill has long been the address of choice for the city's least economically challenged, such as James Clair Flood, who made his millions in mining stocks. Flood's impressive dark brown stone mansion is perched at the top of Nob Hill at 1000 California Street, and is currently the home of the exclusive Pacific-Union Club. Its shell survived the great earthquake of 1906 and the three day fire that followed, largely because it was made of stone. The club took over the property shortly after the earthquake and financed its reconstruction.

Just across the street, to the west, is one of the most beautiful structures in the city, Grace Cathedral. Affiliated with the Episcopal Church, the cathedral plays host to all manner of live classical and jazz performances, and combinations of the two. The exquisite acoustics have made many a musician weep with joy. The cathedral is also home to the well-respected Grace Cathedral Men and Boys Choir that performs during some services and also stages its own concerts.

Nob Hill is also the site of the world-famous Fairmont and Mark Hopkins hotels where you can ride the popular glass elevator up to the Fairmont's Crown Room or enjoy an unparalleled view of the city at the Top of the Mark lounge in the Mark Hopkins. Be prepared, however, to spend money if you plan on dining at either of these lofty locations.

Unless you're coming to San Francisco with the crown jewels, Nob Hill is perhaps not the best place to begin looking for a place to hang your hat. Still, it's a grand place to dream about for when you've banked that second or third million.

Area Code: 415

Zip Codes: Russian Hill, 94109, Nob Hill, 94108

Post Offices: Chinatown Station, 867 Stockton St., 956-3566; Pine St. Station, 1400 Pine St., 284-0755.

Police Station: Central Station, 766 Vallejo St., 553-1532; Community Police on Patrol, 362-4349.

Emergency Hospitals: St. Francis Memorial, 900 Hyde St., 353-6000; California Pacific Medical Center, 2333 Buchanan, 923-3333.

Library: North Beach Branch, 2000 Mason St., 274-0270.

Public Transit: Russian Hill; *MUNI buses* - 1 California, 27 Bryant, 19 Polk, 41 Union, 45 Union-Stockton, 30 Stockton, 83 Pacific. *Cable Cars* - Hyde, Mason and California Street lines. MUNI bus and Cable Cars provide access to BART and MUNI Light Rail stations along Market Street. Nob Hill; *MUNI buses* - 1 California, 3 Jackson, 4 Sutter. *Cable cars* - California, Mason and Hyde lines.

PACIFIC HEIGHTS/MARINA/COW HOLLOW

Boundaries: *Pacific Heights:* **East**, Van Ness Ave.; **North**, Broadway; **West**, Arguello Blvd.; **South**, California and Pine Streets. *Marina:* **East**, Van Ness Ave.; **North**, Marina Blvd.; **West**, Lyon St.; **South**, Lombard. *Cow Hollow:* **East,** Laguna St.; **North,** Greenwich St.; **West,** Divisadero St.; **South,** Vallejo St.

Another of San Francisco's upscale neighborhoods, Pacific Heights is the site of many a grand Victorian mansion rebuilt in the wake of the 1906 earthquake and fire that decimated much of the city. Long the home of some of the country's movers and shakers (former California Governor Jerry Brown once lived here in a remodeled fire station), it now caters to lawyers, doctors, entertainment industry moguls and all manner of corporate big-wig. Affordable rental property is rare here, except in the Cow Hollow area on the northern side of Pacific Heights. Cow Hollow is so-named for the herds of cattle that grazed here in the 1860s.

One of the area's most interesting landmarks is the Octagon House at Gough and Union. This 19th century oddity was built based on the belief, outlined in the book "A Home for All" by Orson Fowler, that eight-sided houses were somehow healthier to live in, perhaps like New Age pyramid power. It is open to the public, but only a few days each month. If you like this house you may also want to look at the 1859 Feusier Octagon House at 1067 Green Street, on Russian Hill. It was named for its first owner, Louis Feusier, a produce merchant.

Finding a parking place in Cow Hollow on weekends is a challenge at best, because that's when visitors flock here to shop in the trendy stores along Union Street between Fillmore and Van Ness. Once the cows were moved out, the area became exclusively residential. Commerce arrived in the late 1950s, turning many ground floor residences into storefronts and restaurants. There's no shortage of options when it comes to cuisine, with everything from Indian (Pasand) and Italian (Prego) to Cajun (Blue Light) and micro-brewed ales and upscale pub food (Union Street Ale House) available. If you're looking for a date, check out Perry's, between Laguna and Buchanan. It's a longtime favorite watering hole for the up-and-coming single guy and gal, and the food's pretty good too.

After the 1906 earthquake and fire, San Franciscans brushed off the ash and rubble and rebuilt their city with astonishing speed. They were so proud of what they had accomplished that they leapt at the opportunity to show off to the world and hosted the 1915 Panama-Pacific Exposition at the west end of the Marina area. The official purpose of the expo was to mark the opening of the Panama Canal. One of architect Bernard Maybeck's claims to fame is the Palace of Fine Arts on Lyon Street between Bay and Jefferson, which was built for the expo. It remains today and houses one of the Bay Area's most popular attractions, The Exploratorium. Much more than just a "hands on" science museum, the Exploratorium is a place where you can get your whole body involved in many of the more than 600 exhibits and demonstrations. Call ahead for reservations at the Tactile Dome, a huge darkened sphere that kids love. Groups have even been known to reserve the Dome privately and explore in the buff! Not a good plan if it's a first date.

If you caught any of the television coverage of the fires that followed the 1989 Loma Prieta earthquake then you've seen the Marina district from the air. This area was hit hard by the 7.1 magnitude temblor that toppled a number of apartment buildings and damaged scores of the most desirable homes in the city, along Marina Boulevard. Most of the repair work is finished, but you'll no doubt be able to see traces of the destruction for years to come, as the owners of these stunning Mediterranean-style homes continue to fix up their lovely abodes.

There are apartment rentals in the Marina, albeit costly ones, as well as one of the liveliest shopping streets in the city, Chestnut. Like Union Street in Cow Hollow (which is just a few blocks south of the Marina), Chestnut bustles every day of the week with a similar mix of shops and eateries and parking problems to match.

The eastern end of the Marina District is taken up by Ft. Mason, a former military facility that is now home to theaters, museums, bookstores, art galleries, public service organizations and one of the world's best vegetarian restaurants, Greens. Reservations are highly recommended here, otherwise the wait might force you to go looking for something else to eat, even meat! On Saturday mornings, a popular public radio program is staged and broadcast at Ft. Mason's Cowell Theatre. It's called "West Coast Live" and it features red-shoed, silky-voiced host, Sedge Thomson, live comedy and music, and interviews with musicians, artists, and authors. It's an entirely enjoyable two hours and the parking is free and plentiful, something virtually unheard of in San Francisco. (Find out more by calling KALW-FM at 415-664-9500). All in all, if you're lucky enough to secure a place in Pacific Heights or the Marina you'll be the envy of many.

Area Code: 415

Zip Codes: Pacific Heights, 94115, Marina, 94123

Post Office: Marina Station, 2055 Lombard Street, 284-0755.

Police Station: Northern Station, 1125 Fillmore Street, 553-1563; Community Police on Patrol, 923-1604.

Emergency Hospitals: California Pacific Medical Center, 2333 Buchanan, 923-3333; St. Francis Memorial Hospital, 900 Hyde Street, 353-6000.

Libraries: Golden Gate Valley Branch, 1801 Green St., 292-2195; Marina Branch, 1890 Chestnut, 292-2150.

Public Transit: Pacific Heights; *MUNI buses* - 1 California, 24 Divisadero, 41 Union, 45 Union-Stockton, 83 Pacific. Marina; *MUNI buses* - 22 Fillmore, 30 Stockton, 41 Union, 45 Union-Stockton.

RICHMOND

Boundaries: **West**, The Great Highway/Pacific Ocean; **North**, Lincoln Park and the Presidio; **East**, Arguello Blvd.; **South**, Fulton Ave. and Golden Gate Park.

Formerly known as "the dunes" and the "Great Sand Waste" because it used to be nothing more than one massive beach, the Richmond is now known for row upon row upon row of unassuming, middle-class, single family homes, except in the mansioned **Sea Cliff** area bordering on the Pacific Ocean to the north. There are few apartment buildings in the Richmond, as residents have long fought to keep developers' bulldozers away. Ethnic diversity, strong family ties, and the work ethic are ways of life in the Richmond, a neighborhood that is populated largely by those of Asian extraction. Residents with roots in Europe, Russia and Israel are also well represented here.

Affordable rental property can be found in the Richmond, although you may wear yourself out unearthing your little gem. Also, keep in mind that when the term "affordable" is bandied about here we're talking San Francisco standards. Having said that, the Richmond, and the Sunset, on the southern side of Golden Gate Park, are two of the few San Francisco locales where you're most likely to strike residential gold, at silver prices.

Weather-wise the Richmond is ground-zero when it comes to fog. We're talking serious fog, and lots of it. It sometimes doesn't just creep in, it tumbles over the otherwise calm landscape with such force that one can almost hear it. And, once it arrives, the fog doesn't seem to have much of a mind to leave any earlier than lunchtime, if at all. Keep in mind, though, that it's possible in San Francisco, due to its so-called "microclimates," to drive just a few blocks or miles to find weather more suitable to your mood.

As you might imagine, because of the Richmond's Asian population, this area is ripe with delicious Chinese, Japanese and Southeast Asian (even Burmese) cuisine. Indian food is also a local favorite here. Apart from the individual restaurants dotting the entire area, there's a high concentration of good places to eat in the Clement Street shopping area between Park Presidio Boulevard on the west and Arguello Boulevard on the east. Clement teems with activity every day of the week as restaurant owners choose their fresh vegetables, spices, herbs, fruit, meats, poultry and fish, as tourists, college students and residents alike drop by hoping to find a literary treasure at Green Apple Used Books, old Moby Grape and Iron Butterfly albums at Recycled Records, pizza at Giorgio's, conversation at one of the area's many coffee bars or Irish pubs, and comedy at an open-mike club. Parking here is atrocious, so if you're not buying so much that you need the car to carry it home, it's best to take the bus and make a day of it.

Sea Cliff, north of the Richmond, sandwiched between Lincoln Park to the west and the Presidio to the east, is not the place to look for your first home in San Francisco, unless you're Robin Williams, who does have a home here. If you watched the television reports about 1996's huge winter storms in Northern California you might have seen pictures of the multi-story Sea Cliff home toppling into a massive sinkhole. The hole's been fixed now, so no other homes are in immediate danger of being eaten by the earth. It's safe to walk the streets here if you'd like to gawk at some of the city's most exclusive homes.

If you like green space, the Richmond may be the place for you. On the north, there's the old Presidio Army Base, which is now a national park, complete with a world class golf course. The base is prime Bay Area real estate, and thanks to the fact that it is now federally protected, it won't be sold off to developers who were chomping at the bit to move in with their bulldozers and blueprints. On the other side of Sea Cliff, also along the Richmond's northern boundary, sits Lincoln Park, complete with hiking trails, ocean-front vistas, the newly remodeled Palace of the Legion of Honor, and another golf course boasting spectacular views. The Richmond is bordered on the south by much-beloved 1000-acre-plus Golden Gate Park. On weekends this park turns into the city's playground, filled with rollerbladers, bikers, hikers, joggers, picnickers, soccer, baseball, touch football and tennis players, and folks who just want to sit quietly and watch those other people fly by. The park also has a Japanese Tea Garden, the California Academy of Sciences, a planetarium, aquarium, art museum, a windmill and live buffalo!

The Richmond was always intended to be a residential area, and that's what it continues to be. It's relatively safe and sane, with all the shopping options one could want either within its boundaries or nearby, and recreational choices galore. Understandably it's one of the best places in town to raise a family.

Area Code: 415

Zip Codes: 94118, 94121

Post Offices: Golden Gate Station, 3245 Geary Blvd., 751-1645; Geary Station, 5654 Geary Blvd, 753-0231.

Police Station: Richmond Station, 461 6th Ave., 553-1385; Community Police on Patrol, 752-0664.

Emergency Hospitals: California Pacific Medical Center, 2333 Buchanan, 923-3333, CPMC standby urgent care, 3700 California Street, 387-8700; UCSF Medical Center, 505 Parnassus, 476-1037; St. Mary's Medical Center, 450 Stanyan, 750-5700.

Library: Richmond Branch, 951 9th Ave., 666-7165.

Public Transportation: *MUNI buses* - 1 California, 2 Clement, 3 Jackson, 4 Sutter, 5 Fulton, 6 Parnassus, 18 46th Ave., 21 Hayes, 29 Sunset, 31 Balboa, 33 Stanyan, 38 Geary.

SUNSET/PARKSIDE

Boundaries: *Sunset:* **North**, Golden Gate Park and Lincoln Way; **West**, Great Highway/Pacific Ocean; **East**, Stanyan St.; **South**, Ortega St. *Parkside:* **North**, Ortega; **West**, Great Highway; **East**, Dewey, Forest Side, Laguna Honda Blvd.; **South**, Sloat Blvd.

Like the Richmond District, the Sunset is primarily residential, although it is also the home to one of the country's premier research hospitals, the University of California at San Francisco Medical Center. This major medical facility is surrounded by single family homes, apartments and flats, many of which are rentals. There are excellent shopping and dining options nearby along Irving Street. This part of the Sunset is often referred to as the "Inner Sunset". Local residents can find just about everything they need here, from daily staples to exotic food. Asian, Italian, and American food abounds, along with coin-operated laundries, electronic stores, and clothing outlets. Many say this is the best area of the city in which to raise children, because of its proximity to a number of parks, beaches, the San Francisco Zoo, schools, and a low crime rate. There is a real family feel in the Sunset.

One block south of Irving is Judah Street, served by one of the main MUNI Light Rail Vehicle (LRV) lines that will take you quickly and quietly into downtown San Francisco, terminating at the Financial District's Embarcadero station. The area is also served by a number of regular bus lines, but the LRV is the way to go, unless you happen to enjoy taking rarely-on-time, graffiti-covered buses driven by often surly "drivers". City officials say they're working on improving MUNI bus service.

There are abundant recreational opportunities in the Sunset, ranging from Ocean Beach along the western edge, the aforementioned San Francisco Zoo on the southwest corner of Parkside, Golden Gate Park along the north, and Sigmund Stern Grove at Sloat and 19th Avenue. Every summer Stern Grove is the site of one of this city's cultural delights. Sunday afternoon music lovers of every stripe cram into this beautiful grove of eucalyptus for the Midsummer Music Festival, that features opera, operetta, symphonic, choral, jazz, pop and Broadway musical performers doing what they do just for the joy of doing it ... and it's all free! If you arrive early you may be able to get one of the picnic tables ... otherwise you'll have to settle for lounging on the hillside lawn on your blanket. The crowds are mixed and that means you could end up sitting between a spike-haired, nose-ringed, bike messenger and a corporate CEO, each equally enraptured by what's happening on the outdoor stage.

19th Avenue is the main north-south artery, slicing through the Sunset and Parkside. It's almost always crammed with vehicles, as it links Highway 280 coming up from San Mateo County and Highway 1 heading toward the Golden Gate Bridge and Marin County to the north. Be aware that its name changes to Park Presidio Boulevard north of Golden Gate Park.

The southern end of 19th Avenue is home to San Francisco State University (UCSF), one of the biggest schools in the California State University System. The San Francisco Conservatory of Music sits at 19th Avenue and Ortega Street. The presence of those institutions means there are lots of students living in the Sunset/Parkside environs which also means there are plenty of local rental options. The best time to find a place is early summer, when many of the students take a year's worth of laundry home to mom and dad's house, vacating their San Francisco digs for someone else. Two upscale neighborhoods border Parkside on the east, **St. Francis Wood** and **Forest Hill**. You won't find rental property in either, but you will find some of the loveliest, best-tended homes in the city. These people are proud of their houses and their neighborhoods, and it shows.

Just south of the UCSF campus you'll find Sutro Tower and Twin Peaks from where, on a clear day you can almost see forever, including the snow-capped Sierra Nevada mountain range 200 miles to the east. Sutro Tower is a strange looking structure, and many would call it an eyesore, but it's an accepted part of the San Francisco skyline. Used by television and radio stations to beam their signals to the masses below, at 981 feet, it is actually the tallest structure in the city. By comparison, the Transamerica pyramid building in the Financial District, comes in second at a paltry 853 feet.

Area Code: 415

Zip Codes: Sunset, 94122; Parkside, 94116

Post Offices: Sunset Station, 1314 22nd Ave., 759-1707; Parkside Station, 1800 Taraval St., 759-1601.

Police Station: Taraval Station, 2345 24th Ave., 553-1612; Community Police on Patrol, 731-0502.

Emergency Hospital: UCSF Medical Center, 505 Parnassus, 476-1037.

Libraries: Merced Branch, 155 Winston Drive, 337-4780, Parkside Branch, 1200 Taraval St., 753-7125.

Public Transportation: Sunset: *MUNI buses* - 6 Parnassus, 18 46th Ave, 29 Sunset, 66 Quintara, 71 Haight/Noriega; *MUNI LRV* - N-Judah. Parkside: *MUNI buses* - 18 46th Ave, 23 Monterey, 28 19th Ave, 29 Sunset, 35 Eureka, 48 Quintara/24th St., 66 Quintara; *MUNI LRV* - L Taraval, K Ingleside, M Oceanview.

HAIGHT ASHBURY/COLE VALLEY

Boundaries: **North**, Grove St.; **East**, Webster St.; **West**, Stanyan St.; **South**, 17th St.

If you still live in the 1960s, or would like to, there's perhaps no better place on the planet in which to do that than right here at the flashpoint of the "Free Love" explosion. Named for the intersection of Haight Street and Ashbury Street, but locally known simply as "the Haight," this area consists primarily of a busy commercial zone surrounded by beautiful Victorian houses, flats, and apartments.

The neighborhood was taken over in the 1950s by the burgeoning Beat Generation who then made way, in the 1960s, for the hippies. You'll find vestiges of both still here, including hippies with flowers in their hair wearing tie-dyed t-shirts and sandals, and bohemian coffee bars frequented by angry young writers with detailed manifestos on how to change all that's wrong with the world. It's also commonplace to be approached on the street by soft-spoken folks selling all manner of illegal drugs. It would actually be surprising *not* to be so approached on Haight.

Had you lived here in the Haight's heyday your neighbors could have been people such as Janis Joplin, members of bands like the Grateful Dead and Jefferson Airplane as well as members of Charles Manson's band of a different type.

The area has also had some very well-to-do residents in the past, perhaps most notably the members of the Spreckels family who made a sweet living in the sugar refining industry. One of two Spreckels mansions in the city is at the west end of the Haight, overlooking Buena Vista Park. The home was built in 1887 and sits at 737 Buena Vista Avenue. If you think this place is grand, take a trip across town to 2080 Washington Street in Pacific Heights and take a look at the other place the Spreckels called "home." Kind of makes one wonder if there are any openings in the sugar refinery biz. Not far away from Buena Vista Park, in the Alamo Square Historic District, along the eastern side of Alamo Square Park, you'll find six of the most beautiful Victorian homes you're likely to find anywhere. Chances are you've seen these brightly-colored "Painted Lady" homes on San Francisco postcards, with the city skyline in the background. Sadly, though, they're not open to the public.

Saturday mornings are especially busy in the Haight, as the former opponents of commercialism do what they can to voluntarily relieve visitors of their cash. If you've been thinking about getting part of your body pierced, but didn't know where to go for the procedure, try Body Manipulations at Fillmore and Haight. The less invasive, but no less popular tattoo is also available here. Used, and often rare, kitchen items are on sale at "Cookin" on Divisadero Street between Page and Oak Streets, an excellent, although not inexpensive, place to equip your new San Francisco kitchen. Here you can purchase everything from non-electric toasters, pasta paraphernalia, china, glassware, and pots and pans, to old cookbooks that are as much fun to read as they are to cook from. Also to be found in the Haight are stores that sell used records, clothes, books, comics, vintage rock-and-roll posters (even some of the "black light" variety), New Age and hippie paraphernalia, incense, body oils and Tarot cards.

Outdoor recreation is nearby, with the Golden Gate Park "panhandle" between Oak and Fell streets from Stanyan to Baker. The panhandle is a finger-like extension of the 1000-plus acre park that stretches all the way out to Ocean Beach. The park, which was once nothing but sand dunes, is laced with walking trails and contains sports fields, playground equipment, an antique carousel, a science museum, an art museum, and much more.

Cole Valley is a small, unofficial neighborhood on the southern edge of Haight Ashbury bounded by Carl and Cole Streets.

Area Code: 415

Zip Code: 94117

Post Office: Clayton St. branch, 554 Clayton St., 621-7445.

Police Station: Park Station, Stanyan and Waller Streets, 553-1061; Community Police on Patrol, 252-0305.

Emergency Hospitals: UCSF Medical Center, 505 Parnassus, 476-1037, St. Mary's Medical Center, 450 Stanyan, 750-5700.

Library: Park branch, 1833 Page St., 666-7155.

Public Transportation: *MUNI buses* - 5 Fulton, 6 Parnassus, 7 Haight, 33 Stanyan, 37 Corbett, 43 Masonic, 21 Hayes, 24 Divisadero, 66 Quintara, 71 Haight-Noriega: *MUNI LRV* - N-Judah.

STONESTOWN/PARK MERCED/INGLESIDE

Boundaries: *Stonestown/Park Merced:* **North**, Sloat Blvd.; **West**, Great Highway/Pacific Ocean; **East**, Junipero Serra Blvd., 19th Ave.; **South**, Daly City/San Mateo County line. *Ingleside:* **North**, Monterey Blvd.; **West**, 19th Ave.; **East**, Interstate 280; **South**, San Mateo County line.

These three neighborhoods meld together and surround the compact campus of San Francisco State University (SFSU) which caters to some 28,000 students. Today the school is known for its Education, Business and Creative Arts departments. In the 1960s, however, it was one of the flashpoints of the student protests. Well known alumnae include actress Annette Benning, pianist Vince Guaraldi (he did the music for the "You're a Good Man, Charlie Brown" cartoon movies), singer Johnny Mathis (rumor has it Mathis quit at SFSU after being told he'd never sing), and author Anne Rice.

The Stonestown area is simply a southern extension of the Parkside district that comes with its own mall, the Stonestown Galleria. This is a shopping destination for people from near and far that boasts major department stores, upscale boutiques, restaurants and coffee shops, a supermarket, movie theaters, medical offices and, perhaps most important in this city, oodles of free parking.

Stonestown is also the name of a pleasant collection of apartments adjacent to the Galleria. There are scores of units here, many of which are occupied by middle aged and older residents who've lived here for years, and by students of nearby San Francisco State University. Just south of the campus is an even larger apartment complex known as Park Merced. Metropolitan Life Insurance Company developed the 200-acre project in 1948. It is heaven for SFSU students, especially if mom and dad are paying the rent for their garden or tower apartment that's just a five minute walk to the campus. Often fog-bound, Park Merced is also home to many families and older residents.

Just across Lake Merced Boulevard, to the west of Park Merced, is Lake Merced, one of San Francisco's main reservoirs, surrounded by a wooded park and the 18-hole Harding Park golf course. Paddle boats and row boats are available for rent.

The western edge of Lake Merced is an area few San Franciscans ever visit, unless they're hangliders destined for the cliffs of Ft. Funston, or they're lucky and well-off enough to have scored one of the delightful, luxury apartments or condominiums lining John Muir Drive. Rents are steep, amenities are exceptional, the atmosphere is serene, and vacancies are rare. But if you don't mind living this far away from the hustle and bustle, keep checking, someone's bound to move out eventually. Some know this area as **Lakeshore**.

On the opposite side of San Francisco State University and 19th Avenue is the Ingleside district. It's a not-unpleasant but lackluster hodge-podge of single-family homes built in the 1920s and 1930s. Ingleside used to be home to one of the city's first racetracks and today Urbano Drive traces the old racecourse. The Ingleside neighborhood is not the safest area of San Francisco, but it is far from being the most dangerous.

Area Code: 415

Zip Codes: Stonestown/Lake Merced, 94132; Ingleside, 94112

Post Offices: Stonestown Station, 565 Buckingham Way, 759-1660; Ingleside Station, 15 Onondaga Ave., 334-0739.

Police Station: Ingleside station, Balboa Park, 553-1603; Community Police on Patrol, 333-3433.

Emergency Hospital: UCSF Medical Center, 505 Parnassus, 476-1037.

Libraries: Merced Branch, 155 Winston Drive, 337-4780; Ingleside Branch, 387 Ashton, 337-4745.

Public Transportation: Stonestown: *MUNI buses* - 17 Park Merced, 18 46th Ave., 23 Monterey, 26 Valencia, 28 19th Ave., 29 Sunset; *MUNI LRV* - M Oceanview. Ingleside: *MUNI buses* - 17 Park Merced, 26 Valencia, 54 Felton; *MUNI LRV* - K Ingleside, M Oceanview. Lake Merced: *MUNI buses* - 18 46th Ave, 88 BART shuttle to nearby Daly City BART station.

GLEN PARK/DIAMOND HEIGHTS

Boundaries: **North**, Clipper St.; **West**, O'Shaughnessy Blvd.; **East**, Dolores St./San Jose Blvd.; **South**, Bosworth St.

Hilly Glen Park is a quaint collection of single family homes, Victorian flats and apartments built along narrow, curvy streets that some say has the feel of a small mountain village. The main shopping area, around Chenery and Diamond, is nestled in the hillside surrounding the Glen Park BART station, making for easy public transit access to and from downtown San Francisco. Rentals are often available in this area, and locals feel this area is one of the city's safest.

The neighborhood is named for nearby Glen Canyon Park, which takes up the sunny bayside slopes of Mt. Davidson. Rumor has it that smugglers from Russia used to frequent the canyon. Few people who live in San Francisco even know this eucalyptus-rich park exists, and because it's not on the beaten path, tourists seldom make their way here. Watch out for the poison oak, though!

Diamond Heights is a hilltop residential area that was developed largely in the 1960s and 1970s. It contains a number of sizable apartment complexes, at least one major shopping center, and some superb views of the city and the bay below. Affordable rental housing can be found here, despite the city's widely-accepted rule of thumb that the higher the elevation the higher the cost. Diamond Heights overlooks Glen Park from the north, and is connected to it by Diamond Heights Blvd.

Area Code: 415

Zip Code: 94131

Post Office: Diamond Heights Station, 5262 Diamond Heights Blvd., 550-6412.

Police Station: Ingleside Station, Balboa Park, 553-1603; Community Police on Patrol, 333-3433.

Emergency Hospitals: San Francisco General, 1001 Potrero Ave.,

206-8111; St. Luke's Hospital, Cesar Chavez and Valencia Streets, 647-8600.

Library: Glen Park branch; 653 Chenery St., 337-4740.

Public Transportation: *MUNI buses* - 23 Monterey, 26 Valencia, 44 O'Shaughnessy, 52 Excelsior; *MUNI LRV* - J Church line; *BART* - Glen Park Station.

THE CASTRO/NOE VALLEY

Boundaries: *Castro:* **North & West**, Market St.; **East**, Dolores St.; **South**, 22nd St. *Noe Valley:* **North**, 22nd St; **West**, Market St and Diamond Heights Blvd.; **South**, 30th St.; **East**, Dolores St.

Much like two identical siblings who've decided to go their separate ways, Noe Valley and "the Castro" couldn't be more different in how they turned out, despite sharing many basic similarities. The Castro occupies a small but vibrant area of the city that spills across Market Street into the Upper Market area, while Noe Valley is a quietly alive residential area just south of the Castro. If the Castro were an opera singer Noe would be jazz.

Formerly known as Eureka Valley, since the 1970s the Castro has been the center of San Francisco's politically powerful and active gay community. For a number of years prior to 1995, Castro Street had been the home of one of the nation's largest and most ribald Halloween celebrations. Castro residents know how to party. Tens of thousands of people dressed to the nines, if dressed at all, crammed into the blocked off street to stand cheek to cheek, to cheek to cheek, as a near-solid block of humanity. However, local residents, business owners and the police have decided the area is too small to host the party anymore. There's no word yet as to where the party will be moved but you can be sure that Halloween will not go unmarked in the Castro.

Castro Street boasts a variety of stylish boutiques selling everything from jewelry, clothing, leather goods, sexual aids, health foods, hamburgers, gourmet burritos, coffees and teas, pastries and more. The Castro also caters to the more mundane needs of everyday life with drug, hardware and grocery stores. Castro Street even has its own movie theater, the beautiful 1930s Spanish Colonial style Castro Theatre, and it is one of the city's cultural landmarks. If you like old movies, including musicals and art flicks, this is the place to go.

Due to AIDS/HIV, which has claimed many lives in this tight-knit community, the free-wheeling days of the Castro seem to be over. Community leaders have naturally been in the vanguard of the effort to convince the government and corporate America to increase AIDS/HIV research funding.

Walk across Market Street, the northern boundary of the Castro and you'll find yourself in the so-called "Upper Market." Almost like a bedroom community for the Castro, Upper Market is a sloping area of well-tended

Victorian homes along steep, often narrow streets. Rentals are rare in this upscale section. Twin Peaks shelters both Upper Market and the Castro, keeping much of the fog away. Many of these homes have sun decks in the back or on the roofs. There's plenty of tight, tanned skin here, and few residents are shy about showing it off. (Note: for an in-depth profile of San Francisco's many gay options, check out the first-rate San Francisco chapter in George Hobica's entertaining book *Gay USA*.)

Noe Valley is inhabited with a mix of middle class families and singles of all persuasion from virtually every corner of the globe. Local comic Marga Gomez characterizes Noe Valley as ambitious and spiritual, sort of a "yuppie Tibet." In general Noe is more conservative than its often-boisterous neighbor, the Castro. The locals are proud of their quiet neighborhood, their homes and their lawns (most of which are very small) and gardens. There's a small town feel here; it's a place where you'd be hard-pressed to find anything major to complain about. Shopping options are about as good here, along 24th Street between Church and Castro, as they are in any other residential area. The San Francisco-standard selection of coffee houses, Irish bars, German specialty shops, mom and pop markets, dry cleaners and other services are available.

To make connections with your neighbors outside of the coffee bars, try the Noe Valley Ministry, a Presbyterian church that also serves as a neighborhood center for information, entertainment and education. Concert fare runs the gamut from religious (it is a church, after all) to jazz, folk and classical. Classes range from belly-dancing to ecology. Noe Valley offers easy access to public transit, including buses and BART.

Area Code: 415

Zip Code: 94114

Post Offices: 18th Street Station, 4304 18th Street, 621-5317; Noe Valley Station, 4083 24th Street, 821-0776.

Police Station: Mission Station, 1240 Valencia, 553-1544; Community Police on Patrol, 647-2767.

Emergency Hospitals: San Francisco General, 1001 Potrero Ave., 206-8111; Davies Medical Center, Castro at Duboce, 565-6060.

Library: Noe Valley, 451 Jersey St., 695-5095.

Public Transportation: *MUNI buses* - 24 Divisadero, 33 Stanyan, 35 Eureka, 48 Quintara-24th; *MUNI LRV* - J Church, K Ingleside, M Oceanview; *BART* - 24th St. Station.

MISSION/BERNAL HEIGHTS

Boundaries: *Mission:* **North**, 16th St.; **East**, Highway 101; **West**, Dolores St.; **South**, Cesar Chavez (formerly Army) St. *Bernal Heights:* **North**, Cesar Chavez St.; **East**, Highway 101; **West**, San Jose Ave.; **South**, Interstate 280/Alemany Blvd.

Named for Mission Dolores, the beautifully maintained Spanish adobe mission that's been at the present 16th Street and Dolores Street location since 1791, the Mission district, or "the Mish," is one of the sunniest neighborhoods in the city. The Mission itself is the oldest building in the city. The original 1776 site, at Camp and Albion Streets, is two blocks east of where the Mission now sits. By the early 1800s, Mission Dolores served nearly two dozen officially recognized Indian tribes, many of whom were forced by the Spanish to give up their homes and live in rancherias. Once interned in these tiny settlements many of the formerly free Indians sickened and died. The Mission's graveyard is said to contain the bodies of as many as 5000 Native Americans. Today, the Mission is where official weather information for San Francisco is gathered by the National Weather Service.

The first non-native residents of the Mission were Spaniards, but the area filled quickly with people of Northern European origin including Germans and Scandinavians, particularly after the 1906 8.3 Richter magnitude earthquake and three-day fire that leveled much of the rest of San Francisco. Surprisingly, only 700 people died in the disaster. The fire was stopped right across the street from Mission Dolores.

Hispanic culture and life reign supreme here again. Mission Street is the venue for the city's annual Cinco de Mayo and Carnaval celebrations, both of which are musically rich, colorful events that are attended by thousands of people from across the Bay Area. As you might expect, the Mission is the place to go if Mexican food is your passion (or weakness). This is a working class neighborhood, and the food is priced accordingly. If you're on a tight budget you can certainly get your fill here and not break the bank. The area is also dotted with dozens of coffee houses, many of which serve excellent breakfasts and lunches with plenty of opportunities for deep, philosophical discussions. Or, just browse through any of the alternative newspapers and magazines readily available in the coffee bars, unbothered by anyone else. Much like the coffee houses of Vienna, many of these establishments are open late and the proprietors won't rush you as you nurse your latte or espresso.

Be aware that the Mission can also be a dangerous place. Walking alone here at night is not advised. This is some of the most hotly contested gang turf in town, and drive-by shootings are not uncommon. Police say if you must walk here alone at night, remain aware of your surroundings at all times and don't dawdle.

Life is a bit more serene just a few blocks west of Mission Street, in the area surrounding Mission Dolores. Dolores Street is a wide, divided residential boulevard with palm trees down its center. The neighborhood boasts some beautiful single-family homes along with plenty of apartment options. Rents here are bit higher than in the rest of the Mission, but they are, in general, lower than in much of the rest of the city. In short, the bargain goes to the apartment-hunter who's willing to do some footwork. Parking is a challenge in the Mission, as it is in the rest of San Francisco, but many properties here have garages.

San Francisco's trauma center is located in the Mission. In fact, San Francisco General Hospital used to be known as Mission Emergency, and you'll still hear some old-timers call it by its former name. No matter what you call it, it is internationally known for its pioneering AIDS care and compassion for those who have the disease. It is perhaps one of the country's finest public hospitals. Nice to have it nearby.

One of the prettiest parks in the city sits on the side of a hill two blocks south of Mission Dolores. Dolores Park is a great place to let the dog, or the kids, run free. However, it is best visited in the daylight hours as gang members are known to frequent the area after the sun goes down.

Bernal Heights is adjacent to the Mission to the south. Named for rancher Jose Bernal who called this area home in the mid-1800s, it used to be known as Nanny Goat Hill because of the goats that once grazed here. It is primarily residential, with street upon street of small, well-maintained, single-family homes built across a number of gentle hills. Bernal Heights boasts some of the city's sunniest weather.

Area Code: 415

Zip Code: 94110

Post Offices: Mission Station, 1198 South Van Ness Ave., 821-0776; Bernal Station, 30 29th St., 695-1703.

Police Station: Mission Station, 1240 Valencia St., 553-1544; Community Police on Patrol, 647-2767.

Emergency Hospital: San Francisco General, 1001 Potrero Ave., 206-8111.

Libraries: Mission branch, 3359 24th St., 695-5090; Bernal branch, 500 Cortland Ave., 695-5160.

Public Transit: *MUNI buses* - 12 Folsom, 14 Mission, 22 Fillmore, 27 Bryant, 33 Stanyan, 67 Bernal Heights, *BART* - 16th St. Station in the Mission.

POTRERO HILL

Boundaries: **North**, 15th St.; **South**, Cesar Chavez St.; **East**, San Francisco Bay; **West**, Highway 101.

Much like its neighbor to the north, the Mission, Potrero Hill is consistently one of the sunniest (and windiest) parts of the city. It is defended from the attacking fog by hills, and offers some of the best views of the bay and the downtown skyline available anywhere in the city.

There's light industry here, along with some small, quaint, hillside single-family homes and modern apartments that seem to consistently bask in sunshine. If you're looking to get into the home-ownership game you may want to scout Potrero Hill for a reasonably-priced fixer-upper that you can sell down the line for a profit. But plan on spending your weekends scraping off old paint and spreading on new, just like many of your neighbors. If you're looking for furniture you may want to check out nearby Showplace Square, one of the West's largest wholesale furniture collections.

There's a real working class feel here, even though many artisans have set up shop in Potrero Hill over the past 15 years. Just as in almost every other San Francisco district, coffee houses dot the neighborhood making it easy for you grab a cup on your way out in the morning. There are also friendly bars for rest, recuperation, and repartee after a hard day of working on the house or at the office, including the popular alternative music emporium known as "Bottom of the Hill" at 17th Street and Missouri.

This is not a place to which tourists are drawn, which is certainly a bonus on those gloriously clear weekend mornings when you'd just like to relax on your hilltop perch and pat yourself on the back for moving to the city that's spread out before you.

Area Code: 415

Zip Code: 94103

Post Office: Brannan St. Station, 460 Brannan St., 543-7729.

Police Station: Potrero Station, 2300 3rd St., 553-1021; Community Police on Patrol, 255-6297.

Emergency Hospital: San Francisco General, 1001 Potrero Ave., 206-8111.

Library: Potrero Branch, 1616 20th St., 285-3022.

Public Transportation: *MUNI buses* - 15 3rd St., 19 Polk, 22 Fillmore, 48 Quintara-24th St., 53 Southern Heights; *CalTrain* - 22nd St. Station.

SOUTH OF MARKET AREA (SOMA)

Boundaries: North and West, Market St.; **West**, Dolores St.; **South**, 16th St.; **East**, San Francisco Bay.

Time was, in the not too distant past, that many well-heeled people would not even consider living in this area, but today SOMA is leading the way in this city's urban revitalization.

While SOMA still contains numerous warehouses and industrial buildings, as well as residential hotels and bars frequented by the down and out, this past is being stripped away and covered over with gleaming new structures, most notably the Moscone Convention Center (named for Mayor George Moscone who was assassinated along with Supervisor Harvey Milk in 1978), and the adjacent Yerba Buena Gardens. The keystone of the local renaissance is the $87,000,000 Museum of Modern Art, designed by Swiss architect Mario Botta. There's also a performing arts complex and the Mexican Museum (currently housed at Ft. Mason, in the Marina district) which is expected to open here in 1998. A Children's Center is also under construction which, when completed sometime in 1998, will include a bowling alley and an ice skating rink. The Moscone Center is also being expanded.

In 1996, San Francisco voters approved Measure B, clearing the way for a privately funded showcase baseball-only stadium for the San Francisco Giants to be located in the Mission's China Basin. Officials hope it will prove as successful as the hugely popular Camden Yards in Baltimore. Plans are to play the first game in the new park in the year 2000, provided funds can be raised in time. A number of waterfront condominium and apartment complexes have been built near the west end of the Bay Bridge, and more are planned. Many of the gracious old red brick buildings built during the area's former glory days (such as the former Hills Brothers Coffee building) have been or are being strengthened against earthquakes and turned into office space.

SOMA also boasts numerous top-name clothing and furniture outlet stores, warehouses-turned-into-lofts for artists, performers and other professionals, bars and night clubs. Singer Boz Skaggs owns Slim's, one of the many nightclubs in this center of the Bay Area music scene, that also features the Club Oasis and The Stud. There are colorful dance clubs, such as the Paradise Lounge and Holy Cow, where you can boogie down until the wee hours of the morning.

Some of the city's best restaurants are here, including the upscale One Market, on the ground floor of the Financial District's One Market Plaza. Would-be movers and shakers take note: this is a place to see and be seen. If less pretentious food is what you're after take a trip to the other end of SOMA to Hamburger Mary's, on Folsom Street. Here the staff does its job on roller skates catering to everyone from Hell's Angels to corporate big-wig all of whom share a passion for the taste of red meat although vegetarian options are available as well. Other top eateries in

SOMA that are frequented by residents and tourists alike include LuLu's, Fringale, Delancey Street Restaurant, Julie's Supper Club, The Fly Trap and Max's Diner.

SOMA is adjacent to the downtown Financial District, and therefore an easy commute if that's where your job takes you. Also, it is home to the city's main transit centers, namely the Transbay bus terminal and the CalTrain station. BART stations line Market Street, SOMA's northern boundary.

Housing opportunities are varied here, ranging from small apartments in wood framed buildings on tiny alleyways, flats in former Victorian homes, spacious lofts, and residential high-rise complex units in the bayfront areas.

Much of SOMA is still not considered safe, and a person unfamiliar with the area may not want to walk around here alone at night. But things are changing, and all indications are that SOMA is fast becoming, if it isn't already, one of "the places to live" in the city.

Area Code: 415

Zip Code: 94103

Post Offices: Bell Bazaar Station, 3030 16th St., 621-6053; Bryant Station, 1600 Bryant St., 621-8646.

Police Station: Southern Station, 850 Bryant, 553-1373, Community Police on Patrol, 553-9191.

Emergency Hospital: San Francisco General, 1001 Potrero Ave., 206-8111.

Public Transportation: *MUNI buses* - 9 San Bruno, 12 Folsom, 14 Mission, 15 3rd St., 26 Valencia, 27 Bryant, 30 Stockton; *MUNI LRV* - all routes along Market Street; *BART* - all trains along Market Street; *CalTrain* - San Francisco Station at 4th and Townsend.

EXCELSIOR/CROCKER AMAZON/ VISITACION VALLEY

Boundaries: *Excelsior:* **West**, Mission St.; **South**, Geneva Ave.; **North**, Alemany Blvd.; **East**, McLaren Park. *Crocker Amazon:* **North and West**, Mission St.; **North and East**, Geneva Ave.; **South**, San Mateo county line/Daly City. *Visitacion Valley:* **West**, McLaren Park; **East**, Highway 101; **South**, San Mateo county line; **North**, Mansell St.

These three areas have much in common. All three neighborhoods are primarily residential and located in the southern third of San Francisco. They are also usually sunny and warm, relatively inexpensive, and are predominantly middle-income working class neighborhoods. Home to a variety of ethnic groups, all three are true melting pots.

The Excelsior is blessed with row upon row of single-family homes, flats, apartment complexes, duplexes and townhouses. Many of the homes are in immaculate condition, while many others need serious attention. This is an area in which you may find a hidden treasure in the form of an affordable, mother-in-law rental unit tucked away in a sun-baked back yard garden. It's an easy commute into downtown San Francisco to the north or into the shopping mall-rich suburbia of San Mateo County to the south. Buses run frequently along Mission, and the Glen Park and Balboa Park BART stations are close by.

Crocker Amazon is directly south of the Excelsior. The homes here are supposed to have served as the inspiration for the Melvina Reynolds song made famous by folk singer Pete Seeger referring to "The little boxes, on a hilltop and they're all made out of ticky tacky." Local kids have the biggest playground in the city, the Crocker Amazon playground. It's a great place, but it's been neglected by the city over the past few years and needs a bit of sprucing up. Residents have been known to mow the park's lawn themselves.

Visitacion Valley is perhaps a bit more lively than Crocker Amazon, but it's by no means exciting. What may be exciting to home seekers is that some of the least expensive homes in the city are here, for purchase or rent, in the form of single stucco houses, wood-framed apartments, Victorian flats, townhouses and duplexes.

McLaren Park, which comes with its own golf course, makes up Visitacion Valley's western border with Excelsior. Crime is a concern in and around the park and there are a couple of public housing projects in the area as well. The world-famous Cow Palace sits a bit to the south of McLaren Park, along Geneva Avenue. The Beatles played at the Cow Palace, as have hundreds of other big-name acts over the years. The arena also plays host to sports and boat shows, dog and cat exhibitions, consumer electronics auctions, car auctions, professional tennis tournaments, motorcycle races and tractor-pulls.

Just across Highway 101 sits 3COM Park (3COM recently bought the rights to put its name on the stadium, to the consternation of many a local sports fan), otherwise known as Candlestick Park, the current home of the San Francisco Giants baseball team and the National Football League's 49ers. This is a cold and windy place, except for a few days in the summer, which is why the Giants are looking to build their own baseball-only facility in the city's China Basin area. The 49ers are working on building a new stadium as well, but they want to stay at Candlestick Point. Their hope is to have their new home up and running by 2001, the year San Francisco will host Super Bowl XXXV.

There's another residential pocket in the city, just north of Visitacion Valley, south of Bernal Heights, called **Portola**. It's similar to Bernal Heights when it comes to housing options, rents, climate and residential makeup. It has a rich Italian and Jewish heritage, much of which survives to this day, especially in the thriving commercial zone along San Bruno Avenue, the district's southern border with Visitacion Valley. Along with the Italian butcher shops, grocers, and flower stores you'll also find businesses run by African-Americans, Asians, Hispanics and Middle-Easterners. There's also a lot of open space here for recreational activities and the aforementioned McLaren Park is nearby.

Area Code: 415

Zip Codes: Excelsior/Crocker Amazon 94112, Visitacion Valley 94134

Post Offices: Excelsior Station, 15 Onondaga Ave., 334-0739; Visitacion Valley, 68 Leland Ave., 333-1150.

Police Stations: Ingleside Station, Balboa Park 553-1603; Community Police on Patrol, 333-3433; Potrero Station, 2300 3rd St., 553-1021; Community Police on Patrol 255-6297.

Emergency Hospital: San Francisco General, 1001 Potrero Ave., 206-8111.

Libraries: Excelsior Branch, 4400 Mission St., 337-4735; Visitacion Valley, 45 Leland Ave., 337-4790.

Public Transportation: Excelsior, *MUNI buses* - 14 Mission, 29 Sunset, 52 Excelsior, 54 Felton. Crocker Amazon, *MUNI buses* - 14 Mission, 43 Masonic, 88 BART shuttle. Visitacion Valley, *MUNI buses* - 9 San Bruno, 15 3rd Street, 29 Sunset, 56 Rutland.

OTHER SAN FRANCISCO AREAS

Two neighborhoods, the **Western Addition** and **Hunter's Point/ Bayview,** were not profiled here because they might not be suitable for newcomers to the city. Since crime rates are believed to be higher here than in much of the rest of the city, it may be advised for new San Franciscans to become familiar with the city before moving to these areas. Nevertheless, according to some, the Western Addition is up and coming and may be much safer in just a few years. Civic leaders are promising redevelopment in both areas but much work needs to be done. Homes sell and rent for less here than just about anywhere else in the city, so you may want to investigate these neighborhoods if you think you might feel comfortable living in them.

SURROUNDING AREAS

If living in San Francisco proper is not for you, there are many other options in the Bay Area. More than 6 million people live in the nine Bay Area counties of **San Francisco, Alameda, Contra Costa, Marin, Sonoma, San Mateo, Napa, Solano,** and **Santa Clara.** Fewer than a million of them live in the city. What follows is an overall look at those counties, divided into four regions, the **North Bay**, the **East Bay,** the **South Bay**, and the **Peninsula**. This information is by no means exhaustive, but it should provide a launching pad from which to set out on your own exploration of the greater Bay Area.

THE NORTH BAY
(Marin, Sonoma, Napa, Solano Counties)

As the name implies, the North Bay is north of San Francisco, across the Golden Gate Bridge.

Marin is a quirky place, filled with every manner of folk, from artists, writers, musicians to CEO's and, truly, everyone in between. There's no telling who your neighbors will be. The county was the subject of a tongue-in-cheek movie a few years back, called "Serial" and, although it was intended to poke fun at the hot-tubbing, peacock-feather waving, affair-having, in-therapy, divorcing stereotypes of the locals, it was not too far from the truth. Life in Marin is more mainstream today, whether or not that's a good thing, although vestiges of the past still can be found, including sixties-era Volkswagen mini-buses decorated with peace signs and batiked curtains and especially in the laid-back attitudes associated with the region.

Much of the western part of Marin is dramatic, wooded mountains and hills, bordering on the Pacific Ocean. California's stunning North Coast begins at Marin, and offers a visual feast all the way up to the Oregon border. Sun worshippers flock to Muir Beach and Stinson Beach on frequently glorious weekends, giving Highway 1 some of the Bay Area's most frustrating traffic problems and making the coastal highway often resemble the proverbial "parking lot."

If you like to hike or camp you may want to make the 90 minute drive to the 66,000-acre Point Reyes National Seashore, north of Stinson Beach. The federal government is working to expand the boundaries of the protected area, by buying up land along the eastern edge, an area that has long been eyed by developers. The seashore curls gracefully around Drake's Bay, so named for the explorer Sir Francis Drake, who "discovered" San Francisco Bay in 1579, even though Native Americans were living here when he arrived. Hundreds of acres of the park were blackened by a huge fire in 1995, sparked by a smoldering campfire. Nearby businesses suffered for a time, as visitors stayed away erroneously believing the entire park had been destroyed. Life is slowly returning to normal, with a serious effort underway to restore the flora and fauna destroyed in the blaze.

If you live in Marin you won't have to go far to take in one of the grandest views of the entire Bay Area, provided the fog has not enveloped Mount Tamalpais. From this wooded vantage point one can frequently see over 100 miles in any direction. The southwestern end of Marin county is taken up by the 1000-acre Golden Gate National Recreation Area, which includes the remains of wartime batteries and bunkers of Ft. Cronkite. Twelve foot guns once sat here, aimed at enemies of the USA who never arrived.

On the eastern side of Highway 101, that slices through Marin County from the Golden Gate Bridge up to and through **Sonoma County,** you'll find the upscale, and highly desirable communities of **Sausalito** and **Tiburon.** Tourists adore cute little Sausalito, and on weekends they virtually overrun Bridgeway, the main street, no matter what the weather. One of the city's best known residents was Sally Stanford. Stanford rose to the exalted office of mayor of Sausalito, despite having run successful bordellos in San Francisco. Stanford also ran a lucrative restaurant in Sausalito called "Valhalla." It's closed now with a new restaurant in its place.

The hills above downtown Sausalito are packed with all manner of abode, from artist's cabin/studios, ranch-style homes, condos, apartments, to Victorians and near-mansions. Rental vacancies are rare and costly when they are available.

Nearby **Tiburon** is perhaps even a bit more upscale than Sausalito, if that's possible. It's certainly more quiet. But this is also where you catch the ferry to Angel Island, a delightful 750-acre state park in San Francisco bay, that is wilderness rich and packed with history. In the early 20th century, Asian immigrants were processed here. Much of the immigration station remains, as does Camp Reynolds, a former military installation. If you're hungry and don't mind spending a bit of money, try Tiburon's Main Street, notably Guaymas. Sam's Anchor Cafe is nearby, also good, and a lot cheaper. Both sport pleasant views of the bay. Life in Tiburon is good ... and residents pay for the privilege.

San Rafael, the largest city in Marin County, is north of Sausalito, Tiburon and Mill Valley, and boasts a mix of blue and white collar residents along with artisans and performers. Rental housing is more plentiful here than in smaller North Bay towns such as Sausalito and Tiburon.

Nestled beneath wooded mountains, San Rafael's claim to fame is the Marin County Civic Center, a national historic landmark, designed in the early 1960s by Frank Lloyd Wright. The building is strange looking, with salmon-colored arches and a blue domed roof at one end, but those who work there say it's a comfortable place in which to earn a living. Much of it is open to the sky and there are plenty of live plants and quiet places in which to take a break. It was featured in George Lucas' 1970's movie "THX-1138"... look for the golden escalator. Speaking of George Lucas, his Skywalker Ranch is located nearby as is Industrial Light and Magic, the high-tech special effects company that creates many of the explosions and space voyages we see on the big screen.

The San Rafael to San Francisco commute can be frustrating if attempted by car on southbound Highway 101. But ferry service is frequent and nearby at the Larkspur Ferry Terminal. On the way out of Larkspur the ferry passes both San Quentin State Prison as well as Alcatraz Island. Drinks and snacks are served on the ride. Buses are also available for getting into San Francisco and back.

Novato is just north of San Rafael. It's classic suburbia, with sprawling malls, theaters, fast food eateries and family restaurants. The sun shines brightly on Novato much of the time. Saxophone giant Clarence Clemons lives here. Perhaps the biggest negative about taking up residence here is the commute to San Francisco. It's even longer and more arduous than the San Francisco commute from San Rafael, although the Larkspur Ferry is an option.

Sonoma County, adjacent to Marin County to the north, consists of rolling, green, tree- or vineyard-covered hills, dramatic coastline, seamless skies, glorious weather (most of the time), some of the world's top chefs, fine locally-produced wines, beers, breads and cheeses, and plenty of room to enjoy all of the above.

The county seat is **Santa Rosa**, 50 miles north of San Francisco. City officials here are picky about the look of new buildings and businesses, so you'll find Santa Rosa easy on the eyes. Despite the close tabs kept on development, Santa Rosa is growing, as is traffic congestion, especially going "cross-town" from east to west or vice versa. Highway 101, which splits the city in two going north and south, is probably too narrow for the enormous number of vehicles it now must handle on a daily basis. Highway officials were not prepared for the influx.

The city of Sonoma, to the southeast of Santa Rosa, is a prime spot in Northern California for just plain good living. A picture-postcard perfect community, rich in history, culinary treasures, and health resorts, Sonoma is a wonderful corner of the world. If you have to get to San Francisco though, plan on at least an hour each way in the car, longer by bus.

Sonoma County, along with neighboring Napa County, is known around the world for its wines. Dozens of wineries dot the countryside, most offering free tastings. Some require that you buy an official wine tasting glass for a couple of dollars, which you get to keep. Visitors from around the country come to the wine country to sample the fare and buy case upon case, often at sizable discounts.

East of Sonoma County, lies **Napa County**, perhaps even more famous wine country. Many of the best wines are made, from vine to bottle, in the Valley of the Moon. On weekends, thousands of wine lovers take to Highway 29, the road that runs north-south through Napa County, stopping along the way at the vineyards, wineries, and picturesque small towns, such as **St. Helena, Rutherford** and **Yountville**. A typical day visit might begin with one or two tastings, followed by a picnic lunch break in a park, then a few more wineries before dinner. If you like wine and you've never visited Napa or Sonoma, it's a delightful way to spend a day.

The city of **Napa** is the center of county government. Hot air ballooning is a popular attraction because of the wonderful weather. **Calistoga**, at the northern end of the Napa Valley, is a popular destination for people needing a mud-bath, herbal wrap, massage, and/or to sit in a mineral bath or sauna. There's also a natural geyser nearby that its owner says acts erratically when the area's about to be hit with an earthquake. Seismologists aren't so sure.

East of Napa county, **Solano** is one of the fastest growing counties in the Bay Area, with housing developments and new businesses spring-ing up from **Vallejo** in the southwestern corner of the county to **Vacaville** and **Fairfield** further inland. Many of the new homes are being snatched up by refugees from the big city crunch. Crime rates are relatively low here and schools, in general, are better than their counterparts in San Francisco and Oakland. Rents and home prices are lower here than in San Francisco, but they are on the rise.

Fairfield plays happy host to Travis Air Force Base, one of the few military installations left open in California in the wake of recent Pentagon cuts. Vacaville's claim to fame is the local state prison that cares for mentally ill inmates.

Fairfield, Vacaville and Vallejo are all typical American towns, with tract homes, apartment complexes, duplexes, townhouses, strip malls, and shopping centers. All lie north-east of San Francisco along Interstate 80 and offer easy access to University of California at Davis and the state capital of Sacramento. Keep going on I-80 and in about two hours you'll be in Sierra Nevada ski country. A bit farther on and you'll be gambling in Reno, a popular weekend destination for many Bay Area residents.

THE EAST BAY
(Contra Costa and Alameda Counties)

The East Bay is the most densely populated region of the Bay Area, from **Crockett** and **Hercules** at the northern end, through **Pinole, Richmond, El Cerrito, Albany, Berkeley, Oakland** and **Alameda** in the center, to **San Leandro, Castro Valley, Hayward, Union City,** and **Fremont** on the southern end and **Livermore, Pleasanton, Dublin, Concord, Walnut Creek, Martinez, Pittsburg** and **Antioch** out east.

The region is so vast that it's difficult to generalize about what life is like here, except to say that it's not San Francisco. For the most part, you'll find parking the car is not as arduous a task as it is in the city, rents are somewhat lower, rental property is more available, and it's usually less foggy than in San Francisco. The entire area is served, and served well, by an extensive criss-crossing network of public transit systems, including buses, trains, and BART. It is also home to one of the most user-friendly big-city airports you're likely to find anywhere in the United States, Oakland International. While officials at San Francisco International and San Jose International are warning passengers that parking lots are full, their Oakland counterparts are usually telling everyone that OAP has space.

All manner of outdoor activities are possible in the East Bay's lush parks, many of which are overseen by the East Bay Regional Parks District. Hiking, biking, boating, picnicking and more are available in the parks, the crown jewel of which is Tilden Park, in the Berkeley hills. Another grand example is Lake Chabot Park in Castro Valley. Oakland's man-made Lake Merritt, spread out beneath the downtown Oakland sky-line, is a haven for joggers, walkers and bikers at all times of the day.

The park that surrounds much of the lake is the site of many public events, most notably the annual June Festival at the Lake, a celebration of the city's rich ethnic mix, with live music, food booths, environmental education, and arts and entertainment booths. A grand time for the whole family, and the weather is usually splendid. The highest peak in the Bay Area is Mount Diablo, located in eastern Contra Costa County. Mt. Diablo is a state park and a popular weekend destination with hikers and those seeking a quiet place to picnic.

The East Bay is home to several fine institutes of higher learning, as is the entire Bay Area. Chief among them, on this side of the bay, is the University of California at Berkeley, or "Cal." The California State University system has a campus in Hayward. Private colleges and universities include Saint Mary's, in the densely-wooded hill community of Moraga, John F. Kennedy University in Orinda, and Mills College in Oakland. The latter is a well respected women's university, that does admit men to some graduate programs. The northern environs of the East Bay are a stone's-throw, if you've got a strong arm, from the University of California at Davis, Sacramento State University and the University of the Pacific in Stockton.

Oakland is home of the National Football League Raiders, Major League Baseball's Athletics (A's), and the Golden State Warriors of the National Basketball Association, all of which play at the Oakland-Alameda County Coliseum complex. That facility is also one of the Bay Area's main concert venues, attracting the biggest names in the entertainment business. UC Berkeley has two more of the area's best attended concert sites: the outdoor Greek Theatre and the indoor Zellerbach Hall.

Oakland has played second-fiddle to San Francisco's first for many years, and often for good reason. But Oakland is pulling itself out of its troubled past, and making a real effort to improve a reputation that in the past has been tarnished by a high crime rate, impoverished areas, and racial tensions. Downtown Oakland's skyline features gleaming new high-rise office buildings, including the dominating twin towers of the Federal Government center. Old Oakland, adjacent to the City Center, is a beautiful collection of Victorian buildings saved from the bulldozer and turned into a lovely shopping area. Oakland is also a world-class port, something that San Francisco is working hard to become again.

Oakland is often in the news, for a wide variety of reasons. Perhaps the most remembered event in recent years was the Oakland Hills firestorm in October 1991. Fire investigators say an arsonist set the fire that raged for days in the hills above the city, destroying thousands of expensive homes along tiny wooded streets that were difficult for firetrucks to navigate. One of the areas hardest hit was the **Montclair** district. Many of the homes that were destroyed in the big fire have been rebuilt, others are still in the process. There are rental properties here, although not many.

Nearby Berkeley is world famous for its top-notch university, intellectual atmosphere, and liberal politics. It is also home of some of the Bay

Area's best restaurants. The city, and its diverse international population, is often so far ahead of the societal curve that it's considered by many to be a bit strange (past nick-names include"Beserkly" and "The People's Republic of Berkeley"). The UC campus spreads out between the downtown area and the Berkeley hills, with some facilities built on those hills as well. Telegraph Avenue begins in downtown Oakland and runs into the southern side of the Cal campus. For the most part, the Berkeley section of Telegraph is a vibrant shopping zone, with clothing, music and book stores, coffee shops, ethnic restaurants and cafes although it has also been the site of raucous student protests.

One of the poshest communities in the East Bay, and indeed the Bay Area, is **Piedmont**, a tiny enclave of mansions, tennis courts, immaculate tree-intensive parks, and civility. Don't go looking for an apartment here, you won't find one. As a matter of fact, rental property of any type is virtually non-existent in Piedmont. If the name Piedmont rings a bell for you it may be because the local high school has for years been the host of a national bird-calling contest, the winners of which were invited to appear on "The Tonight Show," first with Johnny Carson, and more recently with Jay Leno.

Hayward is a sprawling, often hot, expanse of suburbia, complete with standard fare strip malls, shopping centers, gigantic car dealerships, and fast food restaurants. Hayward is mostly blue collar, family-oriented, and largely Hispanic and Asian. California State University at Hayward is perched on a hill to the east of the city, offering higher education and dynamic views of the Bay Area below. The cities of Fremont, Newark and Union City all lie to the south of Hayward, and are similar in appearance, socio-economic components, housing options and the like. **Fremont** is home to the New United Motors (NUMMI) plant, a joint car and truck manufacturing effort by General Motors and Toyota. **Newark** is home to one of the Bay Area's busiest malls, the New Park Mall.

Albany, just north of Berkeley, is one of the Bay Area's best-kept secrets. It's just a mile square, with about 17,000 residents. Local public schools are among the Bay Area's best and parents who live in other cities have been known to stretch the truth a tad in order to get their children into Albany schools. The crime rate is among the lowest in the Bay Area, and it is only 20-30 minutes from downtown San Francisco.

Concord, **Walnut Creek**, **Pleasant Hill**, **Martinez**, **Antioch** and **Pittsburg** are on the eastern side of the East Bay Hills, out where the weather is warm, warmer, warmest. The population is diverse and all economic levels are represented. Housing options are also varied, ranging from massive, gated apartment complexes to duplexes, condominiums and sprawling new landscaped housing developments. Many apartment complexes offer swimming pools and recreation centers. Martinez is the site of naturalist John Muir's historic home, a well-maintained hillside Victorian mansion that is open to the public.

THE PENINSULA (San Mateo County)

San Mateo County sits directly south of San Francisco, taking up all that's left of the thumb of land coming up from the South Bay.

Much of it is middle-income working class suburbia, especially the communities of **San Bruno, Millbrae, Brisbane, Daly City, South San Francisco,** and **Redwood City.** One rung, or maybe two, up the overall economic ladder are **San Mateo, Burlingame,** and **Belmont.** Sitting atop that ladder are **Atherton, Menlo Park,** and **Hillsborough.**

The eastern half of San Mateo County is heavily populated, built up and busy. But the folks who live here have perhaps more options than most Bay Area residents to escape civilization since the western portion of the peninsula consists primarily of wooded mountains, laced with hiking and biking trails, campgrounds, lakes and beaches.

The ocean-side edge of San Mateo County is trimmed with Highway 1, one of the most beautiful roadways in the world, tracing the Pacific coastline from the beach city of **Pacifica** down to **Santa Cruz** and beyond. **Half Moon Bay**, an artsy beachfront community about half way between those two is pumpkin country, and home of the annual Great Pumpkin Contest. Gourd growers from around the world bring their pumpkins and weigh-off against global competitors, hoping to enter the record books. Recent winners have been in the 900-1000 pound range. The downtown area is a hodge-podge of antique shops, clothing boutiques, arts and crafts shops, tiny restaurants and cafes, and cozy bed and breakfasts. A delightful place to live as long as you don't have to commute to distant San Francisco or San Jose.

Pacifica is another of the Bay Area's best-kept secrets, and the locals don't mind if it stays that way. Populated by working class, middle income families and singles who don't mind fog, Pacifica is a delightful beach town, with all the amenities of San Francisco just 10 minutes away by car. Lovely apartments abound here, many of them overlooking the ocean, as do row upon row of single family homes. Pacifica is affordable, quiet, cool, foggy and friendly. Thousands come here each year for the Fog Fest. Beaches are uncrowded, as are the local parks and golf courses.

Daly City is just north of Pacifica, and its northern edge is the boundary with San Francisco. Access to San Francisco is easy, as the Daly City BART station is one of the major points on the system. There are massive parking facilities here, but if you don't get in early you may have to look for a spot on a nearby street. Daly City has one of the area's major shopping centers, Serramonte Center, and is close to a number of other retail centers. Apartments, duplexes, townhouses, condominiums, and single family homes can be found throughout.

Much of the rest of the Peninsula is middle-class suburbia, with the upscale exceptions of **Hillsborough, Atherton** and **Menlo Park.** If you're looking for rental property the latter is certainly your best bet. The other two communities are much-mansioned, with few if any rental opportunities.

San Francisco International Airport is located on the bayside of the Peninsula, in the Millbrae/San Bruno area. BART is expected to build a station in the airport in the near future which will make access much easier. The airport is a madhouse on holiday weekends. Currently, it is undergoing a major remodeling and an expansion of the International Terminal. The Peninsula is also served by the CalTrain commuter service and a number of bus lines. The San Mateo County Board of Supervisors rejected BART service when the system was built more than 25 years ago. Today, most county residents would tell you that was big mistake.

The Peninsula contains a number of universities and colleges, including the College of Notre Dame in Belmont. And, if you live in the center or northern portion of the Peninsula, you will not be far from San Francisco State University. San Mateo County is the also gateway to the Silicon Valley to the south.

THE SOUTH BAY (Santa Clara County)

Rounding things out at the bottom of San Francisco Bay is Santa Clara County, much of which is perhaps best known as "Silicon Valley." Computers, software, communications devices, high-tech weaponry, whatever, it was invented or refined here. It is home of Hewlett-Packard, Apple Computer, and Sun Microsystems to name just a few. IBM has a major presence here, too, with sprawling facilities at a rural site south of suburban San Jose.

Despite recurring fear of a decline in the worldwide sales of personal computers, Silicon Valley is largely responsible for California's recent climb out of years of economic recession. The area is also home to top-notch universities, such as Stanford University in Palo Alto, Santa Clara University and San Jose State University, each of which graduates a large number of innovative minds who go on to found or work for local high tech firms.

San Jose is the Bay Area's largest city. With a population in excess of 800,000 people, larger than that of its most famous neighbor to the north, San Francisco. It is massive urban sprawl, spreading out beneath golden hills and often blazing sunshine. The weather in the South Bay is generally at least a couple of degrees warmer than that of San Francisco.

San Jose continues to spread out, primarily because it has to ... a continuous stream of new residents arrives here daily, attracted by Silicon Valley's high paying technology jobs. Some industry experts say there is a housing shortage in the South Bay, but new housing developments are springing up all the time. Meanwhile, downtown San Jose has undergone a striking transformation in recent years. It's now a pleasant mix of new office towers, upscale restaurants, and shopping areas, served by user-friendly public transit. The downtown area's current big draw is the San Jose Arena, the multi-purpose facility that plays host to the National Hockey League's San Jose Sharks, and big name entertainers from around the world. San Jose is also home to Major League Soccer's San Jose Clash, who played their inaugural season (1996) at Spartan Stadium at San Jose State University. There is speculation that the team will build its own soccer-only stadium, perhaps in nearby **Santa Clara.** San Jose International Airport is centrally located near downtown and, like Oakland Airport, is much easier to use than San Francisco International.

The South Bay is also where you'll find the city of **Sunnyvale,** reputed to be one of the best managed municipalities in the nation. Long-time residents feel their civic leaders listen to them and often incorporate suggestions from the local populace. City officials from around the country have come to Sunnyvale to study how it is run and take home ideas for civic improvement.

One of the loveliest spots in the South Bay is the city of **Los Gatos**, lying in the valley just east of the Santa Cruz Mountains. It's upscale, picture-perfect, wooded, progressive and warm. The city is also centrally located for anyone having to commute into the Silicon Valley or **Santa Cruz**, which is about 40 minutes south over the Santa Cruz Mountains via Highway 17. Other places to check out if the South Bay is where you'd like to live ... **Campbell, Palo Alto, Saratoga, Cupertino** and **Santa Clara.** Campbell and Cupertino, adjacent to San Jose, are similar in appearance, climate, socio-economic composition, shopping opportunities, recreation options, and ethnic make-up. Saratoga is located in the golden hills to the east of Campbell and Cupertino and is almost exclusively upscale in appearance and income levels. Palo Alto, home of Stanford University, is the quintessential upscale college town. The downtown is quaint and busy, and a short walk to the Stanford campus. Rents are high and vacancies rare. The streets of Palo Alto are narrow and tree-lined, and boast some of the most delightful houses in the Bay Area, especially in the older sections of the city on the east side of El Camino Real, a wide north-south thoroughfare that slices the town in two.

SAN FRANCISCO ADDRESS LOCATOR

San Francisco's 43 hills prevented city planners from implementing a grand area-wide roadway grid system, so finding the desired street address here can be a challenge. A good map or atlas is highly recommended. Avoid the small tourist maps; they often distort proportions and exclude big chunks of geography that will prove important to a resident. Transit maps are useful if you're not relying on your car to get around but they don't offer enough detailed information to serve as your primary guidance tool.

City maps are available at stores across the Bay Area, but cartography buffs will want to check out the **Thomas Bros. Maps** store at 550 Jackson Street in San Francisco. The company's *Thomas Guide* is perhaps the most detailed representation of the city you can buy. You can also get maps free from the **American Automobile Association (AAA)** if you're a member. Check your local phone book for the AAA location near you.

With map in hand you may want to spend a few moments locating the major streets and highways listed below.

First there's **Market Street**. It's San Francisco's main downtown street, and it starts just across a plaza from the front of the Ferry Building. As with all east-west running streets that begin at the downtown's eastern edge, address numbers begin there and increase as you head towards the ocean. Market serves as the border between the Financial District, Union Square and Tenderloin areas to the north, and the South of Market (SOMA) district to the south. Street address numbering begins at Market for north-south running streets, with the lowest numbers at Market. On streets north of Market, the numbers increase as you go north. On the other side, the street numbers increase as you travel southward.

Van Ness Avenue runs north-south and begins one block west of 10th Street, crossing Market. It serves as part of the Highway 101 connection to the Golden Gate Bridge, along with **Lombard Street, Marina Boulevard** and **Doyle Drive**. Street numbers increase as you travel northward on Van Ness.

Geary Street splits off from Market in the downtown area, runs east-west, and goes all the way out to the Pacific Ocean, although once it crosses into "the Avenues" its name changes to **Geary Boulevard**. Numbering begins downtown and increases as you go west.

"**The Avenues**" is the locally accepted name for the area served by the numbered roadways in the Richmond District, **3rd Avenue** through **46th Avenue**, and it's important to know because the city also has numbered "streets," **1st Street** through **30th Street**. The avenues also extend down into the Sunset and Parkside districts. The numbered streets begin in the SOMA and run north-south until the Mission District where they run east-west into the Potrero Hill, Bernal Heights, Castro, Noe Valley districts after 14th Street. Thus when someone tells you that the store you want is on "24th" you need to clarify, "24th Street or 24th Avenue?"

19th Avenue is a good roadway to become familiar with since it serves as another connector road, along with **Park Presidio Boulevard**, to the Golden Gate Bridge from **Interstate 280** and **Highway 1**. Both run into the city from San Mateo County to the south. 19th splits off from 280/1 just inside the San Francisco city limits, runs right in front of San Francisco State University, out through the Sunset District and into Golden Gate Park. Its name changes to Park Presidio Boulevard on the northern side of the park. If traffic is really bad on 19th, and it often is, **Sunset Boulevard** is just a few blocks to the west and is usually a good route through the Sunset.

Highway 101 also enters San Francisco from the south, however, it splits off to head for the Oakland-San Francisco Bay Bridge where **Interstate 80** begins. 80 will take you through the northern half of the East Bay, out to Sacramento, the Sierra Nevada, all the way to New York City.

A WORD ABOUT SAFETY

San Francisco, and indeed the Bay Area, suffers from the same problems with crime as does just about every other large American metropolitan area. Because police can't be everywhere all the time, we should be prepared to assume responsibility for our own safety. Fortunately, common sense can reduce your chances of being victimized. Below are a few simple urban safety tips.

- If you feel an area is unsafe, don't go there if you don't have to.
- If you must go into an area that you feel may be unsafe, do it in the daytime and, if possible, with someone else.
- When driving, keep your car doors locked and windows rolled up, and if a stranger knocks on your car window respond with your foot on the accelerator.
- Walk with determination, and remain aware of your surroundings at all times.
- If you're carrying a handbag or backpack do so with the strap across your chest. However, if someone demands what you are carrying, give it up! Your life is much more valuable than anything you're carrying.
- On the street, you do not owe a response to anyone who asks for one. This may seem callous but it is better to err on the side of bad manners rather than bad judgement.
- At all costs, avoid getting into a car with a would-be criminal.
- If you have the misfortune to be a victim of a crime or if you witness a crime, do notify the police immediately. Only if we all do our part will we make this, or any, city safer.

Neighborhood Watch programs are on the increase throughout the Bay Area, but they're not in every community yet. These programs encourage neighbors to get to know each other and watch out for each other, and to notify authorities of anything suspicious. Check with the police department in your neighborhood to find out if a watch program is up and running, and if not how you can go about setting one up.

If your job requires frequent business trips, you may want to consult Stacey Ravel Abarbanel's useful book **Smart Business Travel: How to Stay Safe when You're on the Road** for a variety of helpful safe travel tips.

L OOKING FOR A PLACE to live in San Francisco can be a wonderful adventure but all too often it is just plain discouraging. Chances are you won't be the only applicant for whatever apartment you set your sights on. This chapter is intended to provide you with some basic tools and information that may give you the edge when going up against other potential renters. No guarantees are expressed or implied, but we hope that the information within these pages will help you smoothly find your first apartment in this city by the bay.

San Francisco regularly sits at or near the top of lists ranking the nation's least affordable places to live. Rents are steep and the apartment vacancy rate in the city has been calculated at *less* than 1%. For prospective home buyers, it is worth noting that the median price of a Bay Area home was recently figured to be between $250,000 and $270,000. That's the bad news.

The good news is that salaries are generally higher here than in most other areas of the country, and the local economy is recovering from years of recession brought on by Pentagon cutbacks and military base closures. California has also had more than its fair share of disasters in recent years, most notably the 1989 Loma Prieta earthquake, 1991's Oakland Hills firestorm and Northridge earthquake, and flooding in Northern California that came when raging rainstorms ended years of drought. It has taken years to rebuild, and those efforts are beginning to pay off.

San Francisco's economy has long been service-oriented and tourism-based, and since so many people consider this their favorite city in the nation, if not the world, out-of-towners continue to pour in, dropping lots of cash in their wake. Silicon Valley is also doing banner business in every high-tech area imaginable.

One way you may save money here is on heating or cooling your new home. With year-round temperatures averaging in the 50s-70s, you'll hardly ever have to crank up the heater or the AC unit (most San Francisco homes don't even have air-conditioning). Rarely does it drop below the 40s or rise above the 80s, the exceptions being the few 90-plus days in September's Indian Summer.

When it comes to homes, the city offers a wide variety of architectural styles and configurations. San Francisco's "stars of the show" are its wood-framed Victorian and Queen Anne homes, many of which have been remodeled and turned into flats, with two to four units per building, and a large number of Edwardian apartment buildings with dozens of units. Wood framed buildings — because they give a little when the earth moves beneath them, unlike un-reinforced brick structures that topple — are the safest here in earthquake country, especially if they are built on a solid hill. Un-reinforced brick buildings are deadly in an earthquake, so if you find a nice apartment in one of these, keep looking! Also, if you're especially worried about earthquakes steer clear of homes built on landfill.

There are a couple of rules of thumb you should know before heading out on the great apartment hunt. First, "the farther away from the downtown area it is the cheaper it will be." Second, "the higher up the hill it is, the more expensive it will be."

As with any good rule of thumb, there are of course exceptions. Super expensive apartments can be found in some low-lying areas . . . and there are bargains to be found on the hills. Persistence is the key to finding what you want here, along with the willingness to settle for something less while waiting for your dream home to open up.

DIRECT ACTION

Veteran San Francisco apartment hunters will tell you that perhaps the most effective way to find an apartment in this city is to take to the streets of the neighborhood you'd like to call home, and look for "For Rent" signs in the windows. The notices are often small and hand-written and posted up high. If you spot one in a building you like, jot down the number, call it, and set up a time when you can view the unit. Remember, you are probably not the only person who's called, so the earlier you get to see it, and let the landlord see what a joy you'd be to have as a tenant, the sooner you'll have a return address in San Francisco. You will probably need a current resumé ... yes, this is San Francisco, a resumé ... and proof of income. The competition is fierce and many landlords allow prospective tenants to bid for a unit and then take the one who's willing to pay the most (some may even ask you to pay a year's rent in advance). Admittedly, this "hunt and peck" method may take some time and shoe leather, but many a residential gem has been unearthed this way, and you can save yourself the cost of a rental agent.

RENTAL AGENTS

Paying a rental agent can save you a lot of time — as long as you find a good agent. If you know someone in the area ask if they can recommend a good agent. You may have to shell out a little money for the agent's services, usually a percentage of the first month's rent, or, if you're lucky, the property owner may pick up the fee. The latter would be the exception, rather than the rule. Remember to ask the agent who pays before entering into any binding agreements.

Here's a partial list of some of Bay Area rental agents. Their inclusion is by no means an endorsement.

San Francisco

- **American Property Exchange,** 120 Page St.,800-747-7784 415-863-8484
- **Apartment Network,** 3129 Fillmore St., 415-441-2309
- **Apartments Unlimited,** 2285 Jackson St., 415-771-0447
- **Community Rentals,** 470 Castro St., 415-552-9595 2105 Van Ness Ave., 415-474-2787
- **Metro Rent,** 2021 Fillmore St., 415-563-7368
- **Rental Solutions,**1200 Gough St., 415-929-5100
- **SF Real Estate,** Services150 Lombard St., 415-433-7368
- **Saxe Real Estate,**1188 Franklin St., 415-474-2435 1551 Noriega St., 415-661-8110
- **Trinity Properties,** 333 Bay St., 415-433-3333

East Bay

- **Berkeley Connection,** 2840 College Ave., Berkeley, 510-845-7821
- **Homefinders,** 2158 University Ave., Berkeley, 510-549-6450, 800-400-5588
- **Rental Solutions,** 2213 Dwight Way, Berkeley, 510-644-2522
- **Tenant Finders,** 2110 Oak St., Concord, 510-939-2200

North Bay

- **Marin Rentals,** 305 Miller Ave., Mill Valley, 415-383-1161

Peninsula

- **Rental Solutions,** 437 Cambridge Ave., Palo Alto, 415-473-3000
- **M&M Relocation Center,** 4906 El Camino Real, Los Altos 415-988-0100
- **Corporate Living Network,** Redwood City 415-366-0123

South Bay

- **Bay Rentals,** 3396 Stevens Creek, San Jose, 408-244-4900
- **Corporate Quarters, Inc.,** (short term rentals) 800-698-3238
- **M&M Relocation Center,** 4906 El Camino, Los Altos, 415-988-0100

ROOMMATE SERVICES

If you're moving to the Bay Area alone, but you don't want to live that way, there are quite a few local agencies that will do what they can to put you in touch with someone of like mind to share the rent. Here are a few of them.

San Francisco

- **Rent Net**, World Wide Web page that includes listings for apartment rentals all around the Bay Area. (Use the key/search-word Rentnet to access)
- **Rent Tech,** 4054 18th St., 415-863-7368 (Rent Tech also has a page on the World Wide Web. Use the key/search word Renttech to access. There is a fee to use this service)
- **Roommate Express,** 2269 Chestnut 800-487-8050, 415-928-4530
- **Roommate Resource,** 2285 Jackson St. 415-771-0223
- **Roommate Network,** 3129 Fillmore St. 415-441-2309
- **Roommate Referral Svc.,** 610-A Cole St. 415-626-0606
- **Gay Roommates,** 470 Castro St., 415-552-8868

East Bay

- **Berkeley Connection,** 2840 College Ave., Berkeley, 510-845-7821
- **Roommate Express,** 2340 Broadway, Oakland, 800-487-8050 510-893-4220
- **Roommates,** 1924 Grant Ave., Concord, 510-676-3426

North Bay

- **Share Rentals Unlimited,** 320 W. 3rd St., Santa Rosa, 707-576-0904

South Bay

- **Roommate Express,** 1556 Halford Ave. 800-845-7281 Santa Clara 408-295-5180, 408-727-2077

Peninsula

- **Roommate Express,** 800-845-7821
- **RoommatesBelmont,** 415-592-3771
- **The Rental Place San Bruno,** 415-952-1383
- **HIP-Homesharing,** 364 S. Railroad Ave., San Mateo, 415-348-6660

OTHER PLACES TO LOOK

If you'd rather not pay the roommate referral service fee there are free alternatives, chief among them bulletin boards at universities, colleges, and local coffee houses. If you choose the coffee house route you will probably have to do a bit more initial screening. Many will tell you that the best share rental bulletin board in the city is at the **Rainbow Grocery** in the Mission District at Folsom and 12th Street. It's East Bay equivalent is the board outside the **Whole Foods** supermarket at Ashby and Telegraph Avenues.

NEWSPAPER CLASSIFIED ADS

The Bay Area has no shortage of newspapers full of vacancy ads. This is a good place to begin your search for a home and to get an idea of the price you can expect to pay to live here. Be advised, though, that because of San Francisco's supply-demand imbalance in affordable apartments, many landlords don't feel the need to post vacancies in the papers. Often, by the time a posted vacancy does appear in the paper it's already been snapped up. Having pointed that out, here are the major newspapers around the Bay Area.

- *San Francisco Chronicle,* the most-read newspaper in the area that includes listings for San Francisco, North Bay, East Bay and Peninsula counties and some outlying areas. 415-777-1111
- *San Francisco Examiner*, daily afternoon newspaper that publishes listings similar to the Chronicle. 415-777-2424
- *San Francisco Chronicle/Examiner*, the Sunday paper for both of the above, with the most extensive listings of the week for the Bay Area.
- *Oakland Tribune*, published daily focusing on East Bay listings, especially Oakland, Berkeley, Alameda areas. 510-208-6300
- *Contra Costa County Times,* Published daily with East Bay listings, focusing on Concord, Walnut Creek, Pleasant Hill, Martinez, Richmond, Hercules, Benicia, Antioch, Pittsburg and Bay Point areas. 510-935-2525
- *San Jose Mercury News,* Published daily with the most extensive listings for the South Bay as well as much of the Peninsula and south East Bay. 408-920-5000
- *San Mateo Times*, published daily except Sunday with listings for much of the Peninsula. 415-348-4321
- *Marin Independent Journal,* published daily with listings for Marin, Sonoma and Napa counties. 415-883-8600
- *Santa Rosa Press Democrat*, published daily with listings for Sonoma, Marin and Napa counties. 707-546-2020
- *San Francisco Bay Guardian*, weekly free alternative newspaper with extensive listings for San Francisco and the East Bay. Good for rental and roommate listings. 415-255-3100
- *San Francisco Weekly,* weekly free alternative newspaper with San Francisco listings. Good for rental and roommate listings. 415-541-0700
- *Express,* weekly free alternative newspaper that focuses on the East Bay. Good for rental and roommate listings. 510-540-7400

OTHER RENTAL PUBLICATIONS

Many property owners pay to list their units in glossy guides that are free to prospective renters and available in racks at supermarkets, bus and

BART stations, and on many street corners. These publications are designed to make the property look like the Taj Mahal. Keep in mind that many of them are as nice as they look in the ads ... but some others may not be.

Here are just a few of these publications.

- **Renter's Digest,** 2610 Crow Canyon Rd., #210, San Ramon, CA 94583, 510-552-1052
- **For Rent,** General Number 800-452-0845
- **Magazine,** South Bay 408-988-5811
  East Bay 510-429-7368
- **Bay Area Rental Guide Magazine,** San Francisco 415-929-7777

RENTER'S RIGHTS

There are a number of sources of information on the legalities of being a renter here, perhaps the most comprehensive of which is a book entitled *Tenant's Rights*, published by Berkeley-based Nolo Press, 510-549-1976. Nolo also publishes the *Landlord's Law Book*, for those on the other side of the rental property wall. (You may even want to get both so you know the other guy's rights as well as yours.) Knowing the rights and responsibilities of a tenant and a landlord may prove valuable when it comes time to sign on the dotted line and again when you're ready to move out, as security deposits, apartment cleaning and repairs become potential issues of concern.

If you're in need of help, you can also get information on tenant's rights from a number of offices, including the following;

- **San Francisco Rent Board,** 25 Van Ness Ave., #320, San Francisco, CA 94102, 415-554-9550
- **California State Fair Employment and Housing Department,** 30 Van Ness Ave., San Francisco, CA 94102 415-557-2005, 800-884-1684
- **San Francisco Tenants Union,** 558 Capp St., San Francisco, CA 94110, 415-282-5525

Most Bay Area city governments have an office for dealing with renter/landlord issues. You'll find them listed in the city government section of the White Pages of each city's telephone book.

RENT CONTROL

Once you've secured a place of your own, you should know (though it doesn't apply to all properties) that San Francisco has a Rent Stabilization and Arbitration Ordinance that offers limited protection against outrageous rent increases. Many will tell you that the ordinance is not tough enough, as it allows landlords to boost the rent on vacant units to current market levels, meaning whatever the market will bear. Some charge that the ordinance provides an incentive for landlords to force out long-time tenants to get more money, and to rent units to people they believe will not stay long so that rents can be increased again in short order. In addition, the ordinance does not apply to post-1979 apartment units, some apartment buildings in which the owner is in residence, government regulated housing and short term residential hotels.

For those units covered by the ordinance, landlords are allowed to raise the rent once a year, as long as proper notice is given. The amount by which the rent may be raised is determined by the San Francisco Rent Board and is announced each March. By law it will always be between zero percent and seven percent. This type of rent increase is allowed without further approval from the Rent Board. Higher rent increases do require action by the Rent Board.

LEASES/RENTAL AGREEMENTS

If you want a sneak preview of what the typical lease or rental agreement looks like, take a trip to any well-stocked office supply store. Standard lease/rental agreements are sold in tear-off pads. Of course, the numbers will not have been entered, but you'll at least get a glimpse at how most landlords handle deposits, rent due dates and grace periods, appliances, pets and the like.

A lease of a year or more must be in written form in order to qualify as a legal lease. Every lease must also specify a termination date. If the termination date is not included, the tenant and landlord are considered to have entered into a rental agreement, month-to-month, and such an agreement may be broken at any time by either party, according to California law. Therefore an oral agreement to rent for more than year is considered a rental agreement, *not* a lease. Also, some leases convert to month-to-month rental agreements at the conclusion of the first tenancy period, while some landlords will ask you to sign another year-long lease. Make sure you know what happens to your agreement at the end of the initial rental period, as your tenant rights and responsibilities change from one to the other type of agreement.

If you find yourself in the uncomfortable position of having to break a lease, there are some steps you can take that could make it less contentious and costly to yourself and more palatable to your landlord. Give as much notice, in writing, as possible. If you can, find your unit's next tenant, making sure he or she is financially capable of taking on the responsibility. Until you've been replaced in the unit you will most likely be held responsible for the terms of the lease you're breaking. Keep in mind, the landlord must also make an effort to rent your unit and may not double-dip by accepting rent from an existing and a new tenant at the same time. Local, state and federal authorities do keep a close watch on rentals and how they're administered, but they don't usually get wind of a problem unless someone who's allegedly been victimized reports it. The San Francisco Rent Board governs all eviction proceedings.

It is customary and acceptable for California landlords to demand various combinations of up-front charges before entering into a lease or rental agreement with you. Those charges will likely include a fee for running a credit check, the first month's rent, a security deposit, a key deposit, and maybe even a cleaning fee. If the property manager asks for last month's rent, keep in mind it must be used for just that. That way, when you give your customary 30 days notice of intent to vacate, you're paid up. No lease or rental agreement may include non-refundable deposits. In California all deposits are returnable if all agreed to conditions are met. Landlords are also required to pay five-percent interest on security deposits at the termination of the lease if the unit was held for longer than a year.

RENTER'S INSURANCE

No matter what type of home you eventually set up, it's a good idea to have homeowner's or renter's insurance. Coverages and costs vary but in general, renter's insurance is fairly affordable. Earthquake insurance is a good idea as well, although it's costly and increasingly hard to obtain. Since the State of California began requiring that insurers doing business in California offer quake coverage many companies have stopped writing new homeowner's and renter's insurance policies and some have pulled out of California altogether. Those companies say that quake coverage is too expensive for them to offer because of the likelihood that they'll have to make enormous payouts to claimants. The California Insurance Commissioner has been working on a plan to set up a state-run basic earthquake coverage program for residents. That plan, however, is still just in the formative stages. For up-to-date information on the state-run program, and answers to any other insurance-related questions, contact the **California Department of Insurance** in Los Angeles at 213-897-8921.

So you've got your checkbook and your new apartment ... now what? How about the electricity, the gas, the telephone, the cable? Where to turn for the rest of life's necessities follows.

UTILITIES

Chances are the power is still on in your apartment. That means all you have to do is to call **Pacific Gas & Electric Company** to have it put in your name. The number to call, 24 hours a day, is 800-743-5000. If you're speech- or hearing-impaired the TDD/TTY number is 800-652-4712, also 24 hours.

As the company's name indicates, it also takes care of the natural gas that heats your water and perhaps your stove. Turn on the hot water tap to make sure the water heater is on. If it is, now might be a lovely time for a long hot bath. If it isn't, you'll want to find out why. If the water heater is in your unit, check to see if the pilot light is on. If it's not, follow directions on the heater for lighting or relighting the flame, or, if you're nervous about doing it yourself, call your landlord or PG&E and have them do the dirty work. While you're looking at the water heater, check to see if it is strapped to the wall. This is one of the main components of earthquake prepared-ness (more later in this book). Many post-quake fires are started by rup-tured gas lines to water heaters. Strapping the heater to the wall is an important safety precaution here in earthquake country.

Most people pay their PG&E bills by mail. There are also numerous drug stores and other neighborhood businesses set up to collect money for PG&E. Customer service representatives should be able to tell you where one is in your area. You may also drop your payments off at any PG&E office. There are two customer service offices in San Francisco, at 863 Clay St., in the Chinatown area, and at 2435 Mission St., in the Mis-sion district.

TELEPHONE

There's only one way to go when it comes to local telephone service throughout the Bay Area and that's **Pacific Bell**, though local competition should emerge in the not-too-distant future. To get your phone installed call 800-773-2355, Monday through Friday 8am-5:30pm and Saturday 8:30am-5pm. You won't have to pay a deposit but PacBell will charge about $35 to turn on the line to your unit. That fee will just be added to your bill, and can be paid in three monthly payments. Basic phone service runs about $11 a month. There is no shortage of additional telephone options, at additional cost, including The Message Center, which acts as your personal answering machine, Call Waiting and Caller ID. Hearing-impaired persons may establish TDD and TTY service by calling 800-772-3140.

When it comes to long distance service, there is a dizzying number of companies getting into this lucrative business, and they are not bashful about going after you. Once you've chosen the service you'd like to use be prepared for a barrage of offers from all of the rest of them. And, beware of an illegal practice called "slamming" in which long distance companies call and offer to switch you from your current provider to them, often sweetening the pot with gifts and/or wild discounts. Beware what you say to phone company telemarketers: you may unintentionally say something that will get you "slammed" and you won't know it until your first bill from your new long distance provider arrives. If it happens call Pacific Bell ... they'll take it from there or tell you how to get your preferred provider back.

Here are just a few of the long-distance service providers available in the Bay Area.

- **Ameritel** 800-799-7727
- **AT&T** 800-222-0300
- **MCI** 800-950-5555
- **Sprint** 800-877-7746
- **Working Assets** 800-548-2567

Cellular Phones and Paging Services

They're not just for doctors and drug dealers anymore. It seems as though everyone in urban California carries a cell-phone or wears a pager these high-tech days. Some schools have actually had to restrict students from wearing pagers on campus, even though many parents give them to their children in order to keep in some kind of contact with them while they're at work. Cellular phones and pagers are available from national retailers such as Radio Shack, Sears, J.C. Penney, Target, The Good Guys and Circuit City and smaller specialty outlets. You have fewer choices when it comes to cellular service. Currently the only two companies provide local cell phone service are:

- **CellularONE** 800-424-1999
- **GTE MobileNet** 800-424-3636

Most businesses that sell cellular phones can also activate them for you on the spot, saving you the trouble of having to call the service provider yourself. Some even give you the phone for free, yes free, *if* you sign up and pay for a service contract with the company they represent.

Setting up pager service is even easier, and the equipment is available to rent or to buy. Here are a few of the companies standing by ready to help you get "beeped."

- **AT&T** 800-343-5310
- **Airtouch** 800-677-6816
- **Mobilecom** 800-879-7585
- **Mobilemedia** 800-437-2337
- **PageMart** 800-399-2337
- **PageNet** 800-322-7243
- **Skytel** 800-858-4338

IN CASE OF COMPLAINTS AGAINST UTILITIES

Utility rates and practices are governed by the state Public Utilities Commission (PUC) and, in San Francisco, the San Francisco Public Utilities Commission. The former deals with issues relating to telephone, electric and gas service. The latter handles water questions only. Officials at both organizations strongly suggest you take your complaints first to the utility involved. If you don't get satisfaction there, then the PUCs would like to hear from you.

- **California PUC,** 505 Van Ness Ave., San Francisco 94109, 415-703-1282
- **San Francisco PUC,** 1155 Market St., San Francisco 94103 415-554-7316

Problems with the PUC? There is a public watchdog organization that keeps tabs on the effectiveness of each of the PUCs. It's called **Toward Utility Rate Normalization**, or TURN, and it carries a critical big stick. If you don't get what you need from either PUC you may want to turn to TURN.

- **TURN**, 625 Polk St., San Francisco 94109, 415-929-8876 800-355-8876

GARBAGE/RECYCLING

Apartment dwellers usually don't have to pay for garbage pickup in San Francisco because that is the responsibility of the building owner or manager. If you end up renting a house chances are you will have to factor garbage collection into your monthly expenditures, and your collection fee will be based on how many trash cans you fill up each week. To set up garbage collection in San Francisco call:

- **Sunset Scavenger** 415-330-1300
- **Golden Gate Disposal** 415-626-4000

Outside of San Francisco:

Marin County
- **Marin Sanitary Services** 415-456-2601
San Mateo County
- **BFI** 415-592-2411
Santa Clara County
- **BFI** 408-432-1234
Contra Costa County
- **BFI** 510-685-4711
Alameda County (north)
- **Waste Management** 510-430-8509
Alameda County (south)
- **BFI** 510-657-3500
- **East Bay Disposal** 510-797-0440

Curbside recycling collection is available throughout the Bay Area and is generally included in the cost of your other garbage pickup. In San Francisco residents of apartment buildings with fewer than five units are responsible for picking up the approved plastic containers themselves. Landlords are responsible for setting up recycling programs if the building has five or more units. Landfill space is scarce in the Bay Area, making recycling all the more important. To find out more about recycling in San Francisco call:

- **SF Recycling Program** 415-554-3400
- **Household Hazardous Waste** 415-554-4333

If you decide to settle outside of San Francisco proper look in the Pacific Bell Yellow Pages for the telephone number of your city's recycling program. The folks at city hall should be able to inform you.

If you'd like to deliver recyclables to collection centers that will pay you for them, the **California Integrated Waste Management Board** has set up a hotline that provides the addresses and hours of operation of the centers throughout the area. That number is 1-800-553-2962. For information specifically dealing with beverage container collection centers call the **California Department of Conservation** at 1-800-732-9253.

If you've got a green thumb and you'd like to compost, the ultimate recycle, contact the **San Francisco League of Urban Gardeners** (SLUG) at 415-285-7585. They call it the ROT-line, as opposed to a HOT-line. In the East Bay the **Alameda County Waste Management Authority's Home Composting Education Program** can get you started. That number is 510-635-6275.

DRIVER'S LICENSES, AUTOMOBILE REGISTRATION, PHOTO ID

Driver's Licenses

New arrivals from out-of-state who want to drive in California have ten days in which to notify the Department of Motor Vehicles (DMV) and to apply for a new driver's license. If you're late the cost goes up. The folks at the DMV will want to see your current driver's license, and a birth certificate or passport, for proof of age. Provided your out-of-state license has not expired, you won't be asked to take any written or driving tests, but your eyesight will be checked. A driver's license costs $12 and it is good for up to four years, expiring on your birth date. If you are moving to the Bay Area from within California, you have ten days to notify the DMV of your address change.

Car Registration

If you bring a car into the state of California, the DMV will give you 20 days to apply for California license plates. The DMV keeps close tabs on your vehicle's smog equipment and will want to know that emission control devices on your car are operating correctly. You may want to get your car smog-tested before applying for your new plates. Most service stations will do the test for less than $50. If your car passes you'll get a certificate that says just that, satisfying the DMV. That accomplished, gather up your current registration and smog certificate and take them to the DMV. Bring your checkbook, too. The current one-time fee for registering 1975 or newer gasoline-powered vehicles, and diesel-fueled vehicles made since 1980 from out of state, is $300, a $47 miscellaneous fee, and 2% of the vehicle's value. Registration is good for one year, and subsequent registrations are less expensive.

All California drivers are required by law to carry liability insurance for their vehicles, although you do not have to prove it when you register it at the DMV, as is required in some states. There are efforts underway to require proof of insurance at registration but it's by no means a done deal. Some estimate that 30-40% of the drivers on California roads are there without proper coverage. All the more reason to have it yourself.

ID

The DMV also handles the issuance of state identification cards. In order to get one you'll need a birth certificate, your Social Security card, and $6.

Bay Area DMV Offices

Lines at the DMV are notoriously long and frustratingly slow, but you don't have to stand in them. No, you don't get cuts because you're new here, but you can make an appointment. Call the DMV office you want to do business with and they'll set you up. Then show up early—not late—they won't wait for you! Hours vary slightly from office to office, but in general they're open from 8am to 5pm, Monday through Friday. Daly City, El Cerrito and Fremont offices are open Saturdays from 8am to 5pm.

San Francisco
1377 Fell St., 415-557-1179

East Bay
Concord, 2075 Meridian Park Blvd., 510-671-2876
El Cerrito, 6400 Manila Ave., 510-235-9171
Fremont, 4287 Central Ave., 510-797-0515
Hayward,150 Jackson St., 510-537-6723
Oakland, 501 85th Ave., 510-568-0964
5300 Claremont Ave., 510-450-3670
Walnut Creek, 1910 N. Broadway, 510-935-4464

Peninsula
Daly City, 1500 Sullivan Ave., 415-755-0964, 415-994-5700
Redwood City, 300 Brewster St., 415-368-2837
San Mateo, 425 N. Amphlett, 415-342-5332

South Bay
San Jose, 111 W. Alma St., 408-277-1301

Marin County
Corte Madera, 75 Tamal Vista Blvd., 415-924-5560

PARKING

Vacant parking spaces are some of the most sought-after real estate in the city of San Francisco. Many residential areas offer/require parking permits that allow the holder to park without time limits in the neighborhood. Those without a permit are required to move their cars frequently, usually after two hours. If you're not sure if your neighborhood requires a residential parking permit for on-street parking check for signs posted on the sidewalk. While you're out there check to see when the street sweeper is coming, because you'll want to move your vehicle prior to that time, otherwise your car *will* be towed. Getting it back is a time and money-consuming endeavor, but more about that later.

Residential Parking Permits

The permits are available at 370 Grove St., in the city's Civic Center area. The office is open 7:45am to 4:45pm Monday through Wednesday and Friday, and on Thursday it's open until 6pm. In order to get your permit you need to bring valid car registration that shows your *new* address. That means you'll have to go to DMV first to register your car to your new home. If you don't do that you can get a $10 temporary parking permit that's good for a month. The full-fledged parking permit is good for a year and will set you back $21. You'll also need to bring your lease or rental agreement, or a utility bill, bank statement or auto insurance policy with your name and new address, to prove that you're entitled to park in your neighborhood. Your driver's license is *not* acceptable for that purpose. For more information on the program call 415-554-5000.

Parking Garages and Lots

When it comes to parking in San Francisco's downtown core your choices are limited to streetside meters or parking garages. There are more than ten thousand garage spaces in the downtown area, and they are certainly the most costly option. Fees vary somewhat, however, but, in general, depositing your car in one of these spots will cost $20-$30 a day. Some outdoor lots in the South of Market area will sell you a monthly spot for as little as $100 but more often than not those lots are sold out. Here are just a few of the downtown parking garages:

Portsmouth Square Garage, 733 Kearny St., 500+ spaces
St. Mary's Square Garage, 433 Kearny St., 800+ spaces
Sutter-Stockton Garage, 330 Sutter St., 1800+ spaces
Union Square Garage, 333 Post St., 1100+ spaces
Ellis-O'Farrell Garage, 123 O'Farrell St., 1200+ spaces
Moscone Center Garage, 747 Howard St., 700+ spaces
Fifth and Mission Garage, 5th and Mission , 2600+ spaces

There are many more lots in the city, so if the one you want to patronize is full or closed you'll only need to drive a couple of blocks and you'll probably find one with space. While driving around watch for the much less expensive metered option but make certain you read and understand all the postings. The only people faster at their jobs than the meter-readers are the tow truck operators they call out.

Getting Your Towed Car Back

If your car does get towed in San Francisco, chances are it will be waiting patiently for you at **City Tow**, 1475 Mission Street. The phone number there is 415-621-8605. To win your vehicle's release you must appear in person with a picture identification and be prepared to pay not only the towing cost and ticket but any outstanding parking tickets written against the vehicle. Ouch!

San Francisco Parking Fines

Failure to curb your wheels on a hill	$23
Meter violation	$25
Parking in a red/yellow/white or green zone	$25
Parking on a sidewalk	$25

Removing a chalk mark from tire (first time)	$25
Removing a chalk mark from tire (second time)	$50
Removing a chalk mark from tire (third time)	$75
Failure to move car for street sweeper	$ 25
Parking too long in a residential zone without permit	$ 33
Blocking a driveway	$ 50
Double parking	$ 50
Allowing car alarm to run for 15 minutes	$ 55
Abandoned vehicle	$203
Parking in a bus zone	$250
Parking in a blue (handicapped) zone	$275

Colored Curbs

Red	Don't even think of parking here—it's a fire zone
Yellow	Commercial loading zone only, for times posted
White	Passenger pick-up or drop-off only
Green	Temporary (usually 20-30 minutes) parking only—as posted
Blue	Handicapped parking only, special placard required

VOTER REGISTRATION

Registering to vote in the Bay Area is easy to do. Frequent voter registration drives literally bring the process to you, along downtown San Francisco sidewalks, in malls, and in public transit facilities. You can also register by visiting the Registrar of Voters or Elections Department in the county you live in. In San Francisco it's the **Registrar of Voters** at 633 Folsom St., in the South of Market area. Normally this office is located in City Hall in the Civic Center, but that building is undergoing a massive seismic upgrade that won't be completed until at least sometime in 1998.

You can register with any political party in California, or sign up as an independent. However, keep in mind, that if you don't register Republican or Democrat you are not permitted to vote in either primary election. There is a move underway to allow cross-party voting in primaries but it's a work in progress.

Most California voters cast their ballots in person, but absentee ballots are available if you're going to be out-of-town on election day. More and more voters are taking advantage of this option, even if they're going to be home. If you want to vote absentee you must call your local registrar's office and request the forms. Be sure to give them time to get the forms to you in the mail. Registrar's office staff will be able to tell you what the cutoff date is if you give them a call. It's usually about a month prior to the election in which you're planning to participate.

Here are the locations and phone numbers for voter registration officials in each of the nine Bay Area counties:

- **San Francisco**, 633 Folsom St., 415-554-4375
  Absentee ballot requests, 415-554-4399
- **Alameda,** 1225 Fallon St., Oakland 94612, 510-272-6973
- **Contra Costa,** 524 Main St, Martinez 94553, 510-646-4166
- **Marin,** 3501 Civic Center Drive,San Rafael 94903, 415-499-6456
- **Napa,** 900 Coombs St., Napa 94559, 707-253-4321
- **San Mateo**, 40 Tower Road, San Mateo 94402, 415-312-5222
- **Santa Clara,** 1553 Berger Drive, San Jose 95112, 408-299-8302
- **Solano,** 510 Clay St.,Fairfield 94533, 707-421-6675
- **Sonoma,** 435 Fiscal Drive, Santa Rosa 95406, 707-527-1800

LIBRARY CARDS

San Francisco is home to one of the finest city libraries in the world, with the opening in early 1996 of a gleaming new facility called **New Main**, across the Civic Center plaza from City Hall. The main library not only holds more than a million books, magazines and research tomes, but it also provides access to the Internet and multi-media presentations via dozens of computers. The entire library system's "card catalog" is on computer and accessible at terminals on every floor. New Main is easy to get to as well, sitting just a short walk from the Civic Center BART/MUNI station.

Library cards are free, and you don't even have to be a San Francisco resident to get one. Just bring proper ID, such as a driver's license, and something else with your current address on it, such as a utility bill, and in minutes you'll be carded. The card is usable at all San Francisco library branches. Their addresses and phone numbers are listed in the Neighborhoods section of this book. The phone number for New Main is 415-557-4400.

PASSPORTS

If you really must leave San Francisco for awhile, passports are available through the **Department of State's Passport Office** at 525 Market Street, 2nd floor. It's open Monday through Friday from 9am to 4pm. If you're crunched for time get there when the office opens, as waits of 1-2 hours are not uncommon.

Passports usually take 3-4 weeks to arrive by mail, but can take longer. If you've been called out of town on an emergency, it is possible to get a passport the same day, but it will cost extra for speedy service. The current fee for a new adult passport is $65. You can pay with *exact* cash (they won't make change), check or money order. You will also need to bring a previous passport, if you have one, two identical 2" x 2" photographs, proof of identification (driver's license, state ID card, military ID), and you'll have to fill out the application available at the passport office. Passports are good for ten years.

If you'd like to avoid the long lines at the San Francisco passport office check with the main Post Office in your community, as many of them accept passport applications. Local courthouses may also accept them.

For more detailed passport information, pour yourself a cup of coffee, put your feet up, and call 415-744-4444. This is one of those recordings that will take you through a numbing list of options.

TELEVISION STATIONS

Broadcast television reception in the Bay Area is fairly good, unless you live in a particularly hilly area, in which case hooking up to the cable is the way to go. If you're not interested in cable a standard roof antenna will probably suffice to pull in most of the stations listed below. Apartment dwellers may want to consider getting a pair of "rabbit ears," a small indoor antenna that sits on top of the television set.

Channel	Call Letters	Network	Location
2	KTVU	Fox	Oakland
4	KRON	NBC	SF
5	KPIX	CBS	SF
7	KGO	ABC	SF
9	KQED	PBS	SF
11	KNTV	ABC	San Jose
14	KDTV	Univision	SF
20	KOFY	Independent	SF
26	KTSF	Chinese	SF
36	KICU	Independent	San Jose
44	KHBK	Independent	SF
50	KFTY	Independent	Santa Rosa
54	KTEH	PBS	San Jose
60	KCSM	PBS	San Mateo
66	KPST	Chinese / Home Shopping	SF

CABLE TELEVISION

If broadcast television (those listed above) doesn't provide you with adequate entertainment options, you'll probably need to get cabled. Cable television is available throughout the nine Bay Area counties, with service levels governed by agreements reached with municipalities. Each cable provider offers various packages based on how many channels you wish to receive. Naturally, the more channels you receive, the more you pay.

Here are some of the largest local cable providers and the areas they serve:
- **San Francisco—Viacom Cable,** 800-945-2288
- **San Jose—TCI Cable,** 408-991-1501
- **Oakland—Cable Oakland,** 510-391-3297

• **Peninsula—TCI Cable,** 415-345-1112
• **Marin—Viacom Cable,** 800-436-1999
• **Contra Costa County—Viacom Cable,** 510-432-0364

RADIO STATIONS

There are 80 radio stations located within the nine county Bay Area, 30 AMs and 50 FMs. AM reception is fairly consistent throughout the area, with no special equipment needed. FM reception can be spotty, especially if you live in a hilly area of San Francisco (which is most of the city), the East Bay or North Bay. You may need an FM antenna in those areas. Here are some of the most listened to stations in the Bay Area and their formats.

AM

KABL 960	Oldies
KCBS 740	All News
KDFC 1220	Kidstar Children's Network
KFRC 610	Oldies
KGO 810	News/Talk
KIQI 1010	Spanish
KNOB 1510	Jazz
KNBR 680	Sports/Talk
KNEW 910	Country
KPIX 1550	News/Talk
KSFO 560	Conservative Talk
KSRO 1350	News/Talk

FM

KALW 91.7	News and Information (NPR)
KBAY 100.3	Easy Adult Contemporary
KBGG 98.1	70s Hits
KBLX 102.9	Adult Contemporary
KCSM 91.1	Jazz, News (NPR)
KDFC 102.1	Classical
KFOG 104.5	Rock
KFRC 99.7	Oldies
K101 101.3	Adult Contemporary
KITS 105.3	Modern Rock
KKHI 100.7	Classical
KKSF 103.7	Jazz/New Age
KMEL 106.1	Urban
KOIT 96.5	Light Rock
KOME 98.5	Modern Rock
KPFA 94.1	News/Information/Variety
KPIX 95.7	News/Tal
KQED 88.5	News/Information (NPR)

ALICE 97.3	Modern Adult Contemporary
KRTY 95.3	Country
KSAN 94.9	Country
KSJO 92.3	Rock

ONE OF THE FIRST THINGS you'll want to do when you arrive in the Bay Area is to set up your financial base, in terms of checking and savings accounts. Opening an account is usually painless. Since San Francisco is one of the country's financial centers, there is no shortage of banks, savings and loans, or credit unions. The city is home to two of the nation's largest banks, Bank of America ("B of A") and Wells Fargo Bank. If you happen to pick up an old phone book you may see 1st Interstate Bank listed. Don't bother calling them, Wells Fargo swallowed 1st Interstate in early 1996. There are dozens of other banks in the area, small and large, hundreds of branches, and thousands of automated teller machines.

Most financial institutions offer a variety of account options, from no-fee checking and savings with a sizable minimum balance to inexpensive service if you do all your banking by ATM. There are also more expensive accounts that actually allow you to speak to a human being in the bank or over the phone. If you have time, shop around for the best deal. If you don't have time right off, sign up with one of the big boys, research the other banks and change later if you find a better deal. Keep in mind, that many smaller banks are less expensive, in terms of fees, than their colossal nationwide counterparts while offering you a more navigable bureaucracy to deal with when you need help from your bank.

Note: some of the best financial service deals are offered by credit unions. Ask your employer or other organizations you may be affiliated with (a union, for example) whether credit union membership is available.

CHECKING ACCOUNTS

Setting up a checking account should be no problem, as long as you have picture identification with signature, an address, and some money. Most banks prefer to see that you've had an account at another financial institution before, and they'd love to have your previous account numbers if you still have them. You're likely to be issued temporary checks on the spot for use until your printed ones arrive, usually within a week to ten days. However, most merchants don't like those non-printed ones, so keep some cash on hand just in case. Once the printed ones arrive you'll have no trouble writing checks most places, as long as you have a driver's license or similar picture identification. You should not permit clerks or merchants to use your credit card as check-writing identification. State law forbids that, and violators are subject to fines. Chances are you'll also get your ATM card automatically when you open your account, but if bank personnel don't mention it, go ahead and ask for one. The ATM card usually arrives in the mail in just a few days, ready to use. Most of your accounts can be linked to each other and to the card, making it easy to do your basic banking without ever going into a branch. Today, many ATM cards are also usable in supermarkets, gas stations, fast food restaurants and even at some movie theaters.

SAVINGS ACCOUNTS

Just as easy to set up as a checking account, individual characteristics differ from bank to bank in terms of fees, interest and required minimum balances. Many savings accounts can be linked to checking accounts to provide overdraft protection, usually for a fee. Again, your savings account can easily be accessed with your ATM card, although you'll probably have to ask that it be set up that way.

ON-LINE/TELEPHONE BANKING

Most of the larger banks now offer personal computer access to accounts from home or office, and many more will get on board over the coming months and years in this rapidly changing area. Most of these systems currently use software provided by the banks utilizing programs such as Intuit's Quicken or Microsoft Money. As with checking and savings accounts, fees and services differ from bank to bank, so shop around if you can to find one that best suits your needs. Many banks also offer touch-tone telephone access to your accounts, allowing you to check your balances, make transfers, and even pay some of your bills without having to write a check or spend money on postage. Banks love it when you set up the direct deposit of your paycheck into your account. Some even give you a break on your account fees when you do direct deposit. If you like that idea, ask your employer if the option is available.

Here's a list of some of the biggest banks in the area and their downtown San Francisco main offices. Call them for the address and phone number of neighborhood branches if you'd rather bank closer to home.

- **Bank of America,** 345 Montgomery St., 415-622-2718 (24HR Customer Service), 415-615-4700 (Credit Card Service), 800-227-5458
- **Bank of California,** 400 California St., 415-765-0400
- **Bank of the West,** 295 Bush St., 415-765-4886

- **Coast Federal,** 460 Montgomery St., 415-788-5610
- **Eureka Bank,** 201 Montgomery St., 415-421-6364, 800-538-7352
- **First Nationwide,** 201 California St., 415-398-6441
- **Glendale Federal,** 4 Montgomery St., 415-392-5618
- **Sumitomo Bank,** 300 California St., 415-445-8110
- **Union Bank,** 370 California St., 415-705-7500
  (24HR Customer Service), 800-238-4486
  (Credit Card Service), 800-542-6034
- **Wells Fargo Bank,** 464 California St.415-781-2235

CREDIT CARDS

If you're not bringing a wallet full of credit cards with you, and you'd like to apply for one or more, you'll be happy to know issuers of those cards have simplified the process in recent years. Application forms have become shorter and shorter, and many card issuers will take your application over the telephone.

Here are the major ones.

- **American Express**: Amex offers a number of different cards, each of which requires a minimum annual income and an annual fee. In most cases your Amex balance must be paid in full each month. Call 800-528-4800.
- **Diner's Club**: This card costs $80 per year just for the privilege of having it in your wallet. You'll also need a minimum annual income of $24,000. Call 800-234-6377.
- **Discover Card**: Dean Witter issues this card that actually pays cash back at the end of the each anniversary year, depending on how much you use the card over the period. Call 800-347-2683.
- **VISA/MasterCard**: Banks, S&Ls, and various financial institutions, as well as nearly every other organization imaginable now offer VISA and/or MasterCards, at widely varying interest rates. Shop around for the best interest rate, even if you already have either of these cards. If you can find a better rate than you're currently paying (or one with no annual fee), call your card issuer and let them know —they may cut the rate you're paying now in order to keep your business. It's worth a try!
- **Others:** Oil companies, department stores, home improvement outlets, electronics stores, clothing retailers and many others offer their own credit cards, usually with high interest rates. San Francisco has Macy's, Nordstrom, JC Penney, Mervyns, Brooks Brothers, Eddie Bauer to name just a few that offer credit accounts, many of them instantly with proper identification. One benefit of these types of accounts: the issuer notifies card holders in advance of upcoming sales and specials.

TAXES

Federal Income Tax

The Internal Revenue Service has offices in the Bay Area where you can pick up the forms you need to file your income tax return and get the answers to your tax questions. However, be forewarned that recent studies have found that the answer you get often depends upon the person giving it rather than any clearly defined rule or regulation. The IRS says it is working on standardizing responses. The government is trying to get tax-payers to pose queries by phone and has set up year-round phone numbers to that end. The IRS sets up additional phone numbers prior to the mid-April tax filing deadline and staffs them with additional revenue agents. Many Bay Area post offices stay open until midnight on April 15th to give procrastinators extra time to fill out their return and get it in the mail with the proper postmark. The largest IRS office in the Bay Area is in the twin tower high-rise buildings at 1301 Clay Street in Oakland. There are also IRS facilities in San Francisco at 450 Golden Gate Avenue. The phone numbers for both are the same. For answers to your tax questions call 510-839-1040. To request tax forms call 800-829-3676. Tax forms are also available at most post offices and libraries during filing season (January-April).

State Income Tax

State income tax forms and answers to your state income tax questions can be found at the State Franchise Tax Board offices at 345 Larkin Street in San Francisco or at 1970 Broadway in Oakland. Telephone numbers for both are the same. Monday through Friday, 8am-5pm, call 800-338-0505. TDD access is available at 800-822-6268. State tax filing deadline is the same as for federal taxes, April 15. Tax forms are available at most post offices and libraries during tax season (January-April).

Sales Tax

The local sales tax is 8.25% throughout the Bay Area. It has risen over the years to its current level to help fund the BART transit system and to pay for earthquake damage repairs.

RENTAL SERVICES

In keeping with the business adage "find a need and fill it," just about anything you can imagine can be rented in the Bay Area, from silverware to pagers to televisions and stereos to furniture to wedding wear to steamrollers. If you don't own everything you need to set up house here, have no fear—someone has it and they're ready to rent.

Furniture

There are numerous furniture rental outfits here that will rent anything from one chair to enough furniture and appliances to fill an entire house. Many of them offer "rent-to-own" options, but be forewarned, these can be extremely costly. It will always be less expensive to buy your furniture outright than to go the monthly rent-to-own route.

Before visiting the furniture rental place you've decided upon, measure your living space, and have an idea about where you'll put what. Go in with those measurements in hand and a detailed idea of how many pieces you need. Delivery and setup is usually free and accomplished within 48 hours. Here are just a few of the rental companies in San Francisco.

- **Brook Furniture Rental**, 700 Van Ness Ave., 415-776-0666
- **Central Furniture Rental**, 2301 Mission St., 415-206-7220
- **Cort Furniture Rental**, 1480 Van Ness Ave., 415-771-6115
- **Rent-A-Center**, 3030 Mission St., 415-282-2277
- **Rent-A-Center**, 1375 Fillmore St., 415-567-3313

For furniture rentals outside of San Francisco check the Yellow Pages under "Furniture Rental." Most of the above businesses have additional offices in other cities so you could also call these numbers for referrals to other branches.

Children's Furniture Rental

- **Baby Boom**, 1601 Irving St., 415-564-2666
- **Lullabye Lane**, 570 San Mateo Ave., San Bruno, 415-588-4878

Television and VCR Rental

- **Central Rental**, 2301 Mission St., 415-206-7220
- **Rent-A-Center**, 3030 Mission St., 415-861-0440
  1375 Fillmore St., 415-567-3313
  6298 Mission St., Daly City, 415-757-9034
- **Sunset Richmond TV**, 1885 11th Ave., 415-564-3890

Major Appliance Rental

- **Central Furniture**, 2301 Mission St., 415-206-7220
- **Rent-A-Center**, 1375 Fillmore St., 415-567-3313
  3030 Mission St., 415-282-2277
  6298 Mission St., Daly City, 415-757-9034

Computer Rental and Lease

This being the information age, and the Bay Area being high-tech ground zero, it is understandable that there are so many Yellow Page entries for computer rental companies. Many offer rent-to-own options or lease agreements that come with free or low-cost setup and maintenance packages. Prices vary depending upon rental agency and computer model, so it pays to shop around. Here are a few rental companies and phone numbers to get you going. Most have multiple offices so ask for the location of the one that's most convenient for you.

- **AmeriData**, 800-627-7368
- **Computertime**, 800-459-8080
- **Bit by Bit**, 800-248-2924
- **DCR**, 800-736-8327
- **MicroRent,** 800-444-8780
- **PCR**, 800-473-6872
- **Rent-A-Computer**, 415-398-7800
- **SWA Computers**, 415-692-9210

HOUSE CLEANING SERVICES

As we all work more hours to make ends meet, many find they just don't have the time to keep their humble abode neat and tidy. If you're such a person, you'll be glad to know that there are a whole bunch of people who'd be more than happy to accommodate you, for a fee. There are housekeepers who advertise on coffee-house and university/college billboards, in newspaper classified sections, along with professional house-cleaning services advertised in the Yellow Pages that employ their own workers. There are also referral agencies that will put you in touch with your future housekeeper. Here are a few numbers in San Francisco to get you started.

- **Beauty and the Beast Cleaning Services**, 415-929-2532
- **EURO Housekeeping Personnel,** 415-441-9600
- **Cinderella's Housekeeping,** 415-864-8900
- **Immaculate Connection**, 415-824-2401
- **Marvel Maids**, 415-392-3222
- **Here's Help**, 415-931-4357
- **Maid Perfect**, 415-695-8855

MAIL SERVICES

If you're in between addresses but still need a place to get your mail, there are dozens of businesses that will rent you a mail-box. Many of them offer addresses that sound like street addresses, rather than post office boxes. That's a good thing because many businesses won't take checks that only have a post office box number.

- **Ames Mailboxes,** Noe Valley, 415-282-5008
- **Jet Mail**, Pacific Heights, 415-922-9402
- **Mail Access**, Upper Market/Castro, 415-626-2575
- **Mail Boxes Etc. (MBE)**
  Downtown , 415-495-6963
  Marina district, 415-922-4500
  Nob Hill , 415-441-4954
  Noe Valley, 415-824-1070
  Pacific Heights district, 415-922-6245
  Richmond district , 415-751-6644
  Sunset district , 415-566-2660
- **NetUSA,** South of Market, 415-543-5100
- **Postal Annex**, Lakeside, 415-587-7661
  Richmond district, 415-752-1515
  Downtown, 415-882-1515
  North Beach, 415-772-9022
- **Potrero Mail**, Potrero district, 415-826-8757
- **Safe & Lock**, North Beach, 415-441-7472
- **Union Street Eagle,** Marina/Pacific Hts., 415-921-1850

STORAGE

If you've got too much stuff, or you just need a place to stash some of it until you secure a permanent address, you'll be happy to know there are self-storage units all over the Bay Area. Most are clean, secure, insured and inexpensive. You can rent anything from a locker to your own mini-warehouse. You'll need to bring your own padlock and be prepared to pay first and last month's rent up front. Many will offer special deals to entice you, such as second month free. Here are just a few of the big ones.

- **AAAAA Rent-A-Space**, 3601 Junipero Serra Blvd., Colma, 415-994-4211
- **Army Street Mini Storage,** 1100 26th St., 415-282-0200
- **California Mini Storage**, 890 Penn. Ave., 415-826-7900
- **Crocker's Lockers**, 1400 Folsom St., 415-626-6665
- **U-Haul Storage**, 1575 Bayshore Blvd., 415-467-3830

SERVICES FOR THE HANDICAPPED

Long before there was an *Americans with Disabilities Act*, the Bay Area's sensitivity to the needs of the disabled was raised by a group of handicapped college applicants who fought for admission to the Berkeley campus of the University of California. Their efforts, in the early 1970s, not only achieved the group's goal but they also spawned the **Independent Living Center**. The center, which now boasts offices across the country, fights to protect the rights of the disabled, offers training and rehabilitation services to those with disabilities and offers referrals to support groups and organizations.

    Rose Resnick's Lighthouse for the Blind and Visually Disabled provides assistance, equipment, support and referrals to the visually impaired. Fully-trained guide dogs are available through **Guide Dogs for the Blind**, which is based in Marin County. **The Hearing Society for the Bay Area** provides testing, education, support and referrals to the hearing impaired.

    All BART stations are wheelchair accessible with elevators at every station. Discount tickets are available. Most public transit buses throughout the Bay Area are also equipped to handle wheelchairs, and fares are significantly lower for the disabled. For more information on public transit options for the disabled call the appropriate transit agency (BART, MUNI, AC Transit, SamTrans, CalTrain, listed in the Public Transportation section of this book). Wheelchair rentals are available at a number of Bay Area businesses, the largest of which is **Abbey Home & Healthcare** in San Francisco.

    Here's how to get in touch with the above organizations and a few others in San Francisco (the area code is 415 unless otherwise noted).

- **Abbey Home & Healthcare**, 390 9th St., 864-6999
- **Center for Handicapped Children**, 2000 Van Ness Ave., 771-7057
- **Guide Dogs for the Blind**, 350 Los Ranchitos Rd., San Rafael, 499-4000
- **Hearing Society**, 870 Market St., 3rd Floor, 693-5870
- **Independent Living Center**, 70 10th St., 863-0681
- **Nat'l Assn. for the Visually Handicapped**, 3201 Balboa St., 221-3201

- **Recreation Center for the Handicapped**,
  207 Skyline Blvd., 665-4100
- **Rose Resnick Lighthouse**, 214 Van Ness Ave., 431-1481
- **Support for Families of Children with Disabilities**,
  2601 Mission St., 282-7494

CONSUMER PROTECTION NUMBERS

Got a beef with a merchant or company? There are a number of agencies that monitor consumer-business relations and take action when necessary. Here's where to turn, if you find yourself feeling that you've been short-changed.

- **Better Business Bureau**, 415-243-9999
  Maintains consumer complaint files on local businesses
- **California Attorney General**, 800-952-5225
  Maintains a public inquiry unit that reviews consumer complaints
- **Department of Consumer Complaints**, 800-952-5210
  State agency that investigates consumer complaints
- **SF District Attorney**, 415-553-1814
  Maintains a consumer protection unit that investigates and mediates consumer/business disputes
- **KCBS Call for Action,** 415-478-3300
  Volunteer consumer advocacy service operated by radio station. Hours of operation, 11am - 1pm, M-F.
- **KGO 7 On Your Side**, 415-954-8151
  Volunteer consumer advocacy service operated by television/radio station. Normal business hours.

WITHOUT EXAGGERATION, it is fair to say that the Bay Area is a shopper's paradise. No matter what you're looking for or how much or little you're willing to spend, you can probably find it here. If you don't have a lot money you may be pleased to know that outlet malls are major players in the local shopping scene. Used clothing, furniture and appliances are available at all manner of second-hand stores, from those specializing in one or the other to organizations, such as the Salvation Army, that run their own department stores. Discount shopping is also available from one end of the Bay to the other. If money is of no concern you can be sure you'll have plenty of opportunities to hand it over to a delighted "sales associate" at an upscale emporium.

DEPARTMENT STORES

- **Gumps**: The upscale Grand Dame of San Francisco department stores. Gumps stocks furniture and other home accessories with special attention paid to *objets d'art*, impeccably displayed. The service is top-notch. People come from across the Bay Area each holiday season just to look at the display windows, which often feature animals up for adoption at the SPCA. A treat for the kids. Located at 135 Post St. Call 415-982-1616.
- **JC Penney**: National department store chain that sells just about everything you'd need for your home, including major appliances, televisions, stereos, VCRs, linens, bedding and furniture as well as clothing, shoes, jewelry and cosmetics. Numerous Bay Area locations, but none in San Francisco.

  Daly City, Westlake Shopping Center, 415-756-3000
  East Bay, South Shore Center, 510-521-0211
  Richmond Hilltop Mall, 510-222-4411
- **Macy's**: The Union Square store is reportedly the largest in the nation, outside of the flagship store in Manhattan. You could fully stock your closets and furnish your entire home here if you were so inclined, as Macy's carries clothing, shoes, linens, bedding, appli-

ances, cookware, gourmet items, luggage, and more. Service, once notoriously bad, has improved of late. Bay Area locations include:

   San Francisco, Union Square, Stockton & O'Farrell streets 415-397-3333

   Peninsula, Daly City, 1 Serramonte Center, 415-994-3333

   East Bay, San Leandro, Bayfair Mall, 510-357-3333

   North Bay, San Rafael, Northgate Mall, 415-499-5200

- **Mervyns**: Medium priced department store specializing in clothing, shoes, linens, bedding, home accessories, known for big and frequent sales. Numerous locations across the Bay Area:

   San Francisco, 2675 Geary Blvd., 415-921-0888

   Peninsula, 63 Serramonte Center, 415-756-9022

   East Bay, South Shore Center, Alameda, 510-769-8800

   Southland Mall, Hayward, 510-782-8000

   North Bay, Northgate Mall, San Rafael, 415-499-9330

- **Nordstrom**: Employees at this Seattle-based retailer have a reputation of being helpful, courteous and knowledgeable about the merchandise they sell. That merchandise ranges from shoes and clothing for the entire family to jewelry and cosmetics and more. Perhaps most popular here are the women's shoe sales. Bay Area locations include:

   San Francisco, SF Shopping Centre, 865 Market Street, 415-243-8500

   Stonestown Galleria, 285 Winston Drive, 415-753-1344

   Peninsula, Hillsdale Mall, San Mateo, 415-570-5111

   North Bay, Village @ Corte Madera, 1870 Redwood Hwy., Corte Madera, 415-927-1690

   East Bay, 1200 Broadway Plaza, Walnut Creek, 510-930-7959

- **Saks Fifth Avenue**: Upscale and they know it. Clothing, jewelry, cosmetics, *objets d'art*. Located at 384 Post Street on Union Square. Telephone 415-986-4300.

Discount chains, such as **K-mart**, **Target**, **WalMart** and **Woolworths** all exist in the Bay Area. Check the Yellow Pages for the nearest location of your favorite.

MALLS

San Francisco
- **SF Shopping Centre**, 5th & Market, 415-495-5656
- **Stonestown Galleria**, 3251 20th Ave.415-759-2623

Peninsula
- **Serramonte Center**, Daly City, 415-992-8686
- **Tanforan Park**, San Bruno, 415-873-2000
- **Westlake Shopping Center**, Daly City, 415-756-2161
- **Hillsdale Mall**, San Mateo, 415-345-8222
- **Stanford Shopping Center**, Palo Alto, 415-617-8230

North Bay
- **Northgate Mall**, San Rafael, 415-479-5955
- **Larkspur Landing**, Larkspur, 415-461-0172
- **Village**, Corte Madera, 415-924-8557
- **Town & Country**, Corte Madera, 415-924-2961

East Bay
- **Hilltop Mall**, Richmond, 510-223-1933
- **The Willows**, Concord, 510-825-4000
- **Sun Valley**, Concord, 510-825-2042
- **New Park Mall**, Newark, 510-794-5522
- **South Shore Center**, Alameda, 510-521-1515
- **Bayfair Mall**, San Leandro, 510-357-6000
- **Great Mall of the Bay Area**, Milpitas 408-956-2033

OUTLET MALLS

Whether these places actually offer more affordable merchandise than elsewhere is debatable but what is not questionable is their nationwide popularity and rapid growth. In the following areas try:

- East Bay, **Marina Square**, San Leandro, no main number, 1259 Marina Boulevard
- South Bay, **Pacific Outlet Mall**, Gilroy, 408-847-4155 Highway 101 at Leavesley exit
- North Bay, **Vacaville Commons**, Vacaville, 707-447-0267 2098 Harbison Drive

FURNITURE

There are too many furniture stores in the Bay Area to list them all, but here are a few well-known names to get you started in your search for perfect and affordable home furnishings.

- **Drexel Heritage-Casa Marin Home Furnishings**, 1654 2nd St., San Rafael, 415-454-0502
- **Suburban House**, 1150 Concord Ave., Concord, 510-671-7373
- **Levitz Furniture Warehouse**, 900 Dubuque Ave., South San Francisco, 415-873-6660
- **Henredon-Noriega Furniture**, 1455 Taraval St., San Francisco, 415-564-4110
- **Scandinavian Designs**
  Peninsula, 317-South B St., San Mateo, 415-340-0555
  East Bay, 2101 Shattuck Ave., Berkeley, 510-848-8250
  North Bay, 1212 4th St., San Rafael, 415-457-5500
- **Ethan Allen Galleries**, 1060 Redwood Highway, Mill Valley, 415-383-3600

USED FURNITURE

Shopping for second hand furnishings can be just as much fun as shopping for new. The chances of finding a real treasure shoved into a long-ignored corner of a moving-company run warehouse add to the excitement of saving a bit of cash. Here are a few places at which you may want to begin your adventure.

- **Busvan Bonded Dealers & Appraisers**, Two locations in San Francisco, 900 Front St. and 244 Clement St. Respective phone numbers, 415-981-1405 and 415-752-5353
- **Cort Furniture Rental and Clearance**, 600 Dubuque Ave., South San Francisco, 415-952-9791
- **Cottrell's Moving and Storage**, 150 Valencia St., San Francisco, 415-431-1000
- **Harrington Brothers**, 599 Valencia St., San Francisco, 415-861-7300

ANTIQUES

There are nine pages of antique dealer listings in the San Francisco Yellow Pages alone, but collectible furniture is available in practically every Bay Area city. The 400 block of Jackson Street, in the Financial District, is known for its high concentration of antique stores that could serve as your jumping off point. Most of the Jackson Street dealers are members of the Antique Dealers Association of California, and if they don't have what you're looking for they can perhaps steer you in the right direction.

HARDWARE/PAINTS/WALLPAPER

Everything you might need to fix up your new place is readily available, with most San Francisco neighborhoods having at least one hardware store of its own. If the local store doesn't have that special color of paint you want for the sun porch you can also try one of many cavernous home improvement centers. The stores listed are in San Francisco unless otherwise noted.

ACE Hardware Stores

- **Brownie's Hardware**, 1552 Polk St., 415-673-8900
- **Cole Hardware**, 956 Cole St., 415-753-2653
- **Discount Builders**, 1695 Mission St., 415-621-8511
- **Front Hardware,** 195 Pine St., 415-362-8028
- **Golden Gate Bldg.** , 1333 Pacific Ave., 415-441-0945
- **Standard 5-10-25**, 3545 California St., 415-751-5767
- **Standard Hardware**, 1019 Clement St., 415-221-1888

True Value Hardware Stores

- **Creative Paint** , 5435 Geary Blvd., 415-666-3380
- **Pacific Heights Hardware** 2828 Calif. St., 415-346-9262
- **Progress Hardware**, 724 Irving St., 415-731-2038
- **Sunset Hardware**, 3126 Noriega St., 415-661-0607
- **True Value Hardware**, 220 Taraval St., 415-564-3249
- **True Value Hardware**, 2244 Irving St., 415-753-6862

HOME IMPROVEMENT CENTERS

The big do-it-yourself centers are located outside of San Francisco, but the ones listed below are all within a 15-30 minute drive.

- **Orchard Supply Hardware (OSH)**
  Peninsula, 2245 Gellert Blvd., South San Francisco, 415-878-3322
  900 El Camino Real, Millbrae, 415-873-5536
  North Bay, 1151 Anderson Drive, San Rafael, 415-453-7288
  East Bay, 1025 Ashby Ave., Berkeley, 510-540-6638
- **Home Depot**
  Peninsula, 91 Colma Blvd., Colma, 415-992-9600
  East Bay, 1933 Davis St., San Leandro, 510-636-9600
  11955 San Pablo Ave., El Ceritto, 510-235-0800
- **Yardbirds**
  East Bay, 13901 San Pablo Ave., San Pablo, 510-236-4630
  North Bay, 1801 4th St., San Rafael, 415-457-5880

ELECTRONICS/APPLIANCES

There are dozens of individually owned and operated electronics and appliance stores throughout the Bay Area as well as all the familiar national chain retailers. To find what you're looking for close to your home, check the Pacific Bell Yellow Pages. Here are a few of those businesses, located in San Francisco unless otherwise noted.

- **Circuit City**, 1200 Van Ness Ave., 415-441-1300
- **Good Guys**, 1400 Van Ness Ave., 415-775-9323
- **Whole Earth Access**, 401 Bayshore Blvd., 415-285-5244
- **Montgomery Wards**, Serramonte Center, Daly City, 415-991-6268
- **Sears**, Tanforan Mall, San Bruno, 415-244-5022

USED HOUSEWARES/APPLIANCES

- **Cookin'**, 339 Divisadero St., 415-861-1854

COMPUTERS

Again, Bay Area Yellow Pages devote a lot of space to computers, so you may want to begin your search at one of these big name stores to get a feel for prices and options. Then, if you don't find what you want there, you can hit the streets armed with some background information that may prove useful wherever you decide to buy. Locations are in San Francisco unless otherwise noted.

- **Circuit City,** 1200 Van Ness Ave., 415-441-1300
- **Good Guys**, 1400 Van Ness Ave., 415-775-9323
- **CompUSA**, 1250 El Camino Real, San Bruno, 415-244-9980
  3839 Emery, Emeryville, 510-450-9500
- **Fry's**, 600 Hamilton Ave., Campbell, 408-364-3700
- **Whole Earth Access** 401 Bayshore Blvd., 415-285-5244

Another good place to look for computer information is *Computer Currents* magazine. It comes out bi-weekly and is free. Look for it on streetside racks throughout the Bay Area or contact them at 510-547-6800 or on the Internet at http://www.currents.net.

BEDS AND BEDDING

Most, if not all, of San Francisco's department stores deal in bedding, and many of them sell beds as well. For their names, locations and phone numbers see the previous entries under "Department Stores." Also check listings under "Furniture." Here's a list of just some of the San Francisco stores that deal exclusively in these items.

- **Beds and Bedding**, 5036 Geary Blvd., 415-387-1684
- **Discount Depot**, 520 Haight St., 415-552-9279
- **Dreams Inc.**, 921 Howard St., 415-543-1800
- **Duxiana**, 1803 Fillmore St., 415-673-7134
- **Futon Shop**, 810 Van Ness Ave., 415-56-FUTON
- **Oysterbeds,** 17th & DeHaro St., 415-626-4343
- **Scheuer Linens,** 340 Sutter St., 415-392-2813
- **Warm Things**, 3063 Fillmore St., 415-931-1660

HOUSEWARES

Department stores carry dishes, glassware, and most other items needed for the home, so if you have a favorite that may be the place to start. There are also numerous specialty outlets from which to choose, including the following, located in San Francisco unless otherwise noted.

- **Crate & Barrel,** 125 Grant Ave., 415-986-4000
- **Lechter's**, 3251 20th Ave., 415-759-0528

24 Serramonte Center, Daly City, 415-992-5047
- **Pottery Barn,** 1 Embarcadero Center , 415-788-6810
- **Williams Sonoma**, 865 Market St., 415-546-0171
  150 Post St., 415-362-6904
  2 Embarcadero Center, 415-421-2033
  Stonestown Galleria, 415-681-5525

CARPETS

- **Armstrong Carpets**, 626 Clement St., 415-751-2827
- **Carpet Connection,** 390 Bayshore Blvd., 415-550-7125
- **Conklin Brothers**, 1100 Selby , 415-282-1822
- **MMM Carpets**, 375 Gellert Blvd., Daly City, 415-994-4000

RUGS

- **Cost Plus Imports**, 2552 Taylor St., 415-928-6200
  785 Serramonte Blvd., Daly City, 415-994-7090
  201 Clay St., Oakland, 510-893-7300
- **Pier One Imports,** 2275 Market St., 415-431-8144
  3535 Geary Blvd., 415-387-6642
  101 Gellert Blvd., Colma, 415-755-6600

GROCERIES

The Bay Area is blessed with a wide selection of supermarket chains that range from inexpensive to downright exorbitant. The budget grocery stores offer bulk quantities of your average fare while the more expensive stores emphasize fresh produce, organics and imported goods. The big grocery chains fall in between those two extremes. For budget shopping head for **Foods Co., Food 4-Less, Grocery Outlet, Smart and Final** and **Pak-N-Save. Bell Markets, Lucky, Safeway** and **SaveMart** are the next rung up the ladder. **Andronico's** reigns supreme at the high end.

San Francisco is surrounded by some of the most productive farmland in the world (the San Joaquin Valley, and the counties of Sonoma, Salinas and Monterey). Many of the men and women who till those farms take at least one day a week to hawk the fruits and vegetables of their labors at **Farmer's Markets** all around the Bay Area. Organic produce is also available and most sellers will offer you a taste before you buy. Here's a list of some of the markets held in or close to San Francisco.

San Francisco

- **100 Alemany Blvd.,** Saturday, dawn to dusk, year round
- **Ferry Plaza on the Embarcadero,** Saturday, 9am-2pm, year round
- **United Nation's Plaza,** Market St. (between 7th and 8th Streets), Sunday and, Wednesday, 7am-5pm, year round

Marin County

- **Corte Madera:** Village Shopping Center, Wednesday, 3pm-dusk, May-October
- **Novato:** Downtown (Sherman Avenue between Grant and Delong Avenues), Tuesday, 4pm-8pm, May to October
- **San Rafael:** Downtown (4th at B St.), Thursday, 6pm-9pm, April-October
- **San Rafael:** Marin Civic Center, Sunday and Thursday, 8am-1pm, year round

San Mateo County

- **Daly City:** Serramonte Center, Thursday, 10am-2pm, year round
- **Menlo Park:** Downtown Parking Plaza, Sunday, 10am-2pm, May-November
- **Millbrae:** 200 Broadway, Saturday, 8am-1pm, year round

Alameda County

- **Berkeley:** Center Street at MLK Way, Saturday, 10am-2pm, year round
- **Oakland:** Jack London Square, Sunday, 10am-2pm, year round
- **El Cerrito:** El Cerrito Plaza, Tuesday, 9am-1pm, year round

WAREHOUSE SHOPPING

Two giants in the club-shopping business have merged creating **Price-Costco**, cavernous warehouse-type facilities stacked from floor to ceiling with restaurant-trade items, such as gallon jars of olives, mayonnaise, six-packs of everything from chopped tomatoes to pet food, tires, cleaning supplies, clothing and pharmaceuticals. Basic membership costs $35 a year, and there are numerous locations around the Bay Area. The San Francisco store is at 450 10th Street, 415-626-4341.

SECOND-HAND/VINTAGE CLOTHES

Your mother might call it second-hand but today that pair of 1970 elephant bottoms in the bottom of a box in the basement may have become high fashion "vintage" to an aficionado. In San Francisco, dressing in stylish cast-offs has been all the rage for some time and there are scores of stores specializing in it. There are also plenty of shops that sell second-hand items that don't quite qualify as vintage. Vintage is consistently more expensive than second-hand and usually in pristine condition. Here are some places to start.

- **Attic Shop**, 1040 Hyde St., 415-474-3498
- **Cathedral School**, 1036 Hyde St., 415-776-6630
- **Discovery Shop**, 1827 Union St., 415-929-8053

- **Goodwill**, 1500 Mission St., 415-550-4500
  (main office, numerous locations)
- **Repeat Performance** , 2223 Fillmore St., 415-563-3123
- **Salvation Army,** 1185 Sutter St., 415-771-3818
- **St. Vincent de Paul,** 1745 Folsom St., 415-626-1515
  1519 Haight St., 415-863-3615
  186 W. Portal Ave., 415-664-7119
- **Thrift Town**, 2101 Mission St., 415-861-1132
- **Town School Closet**, 3325 Sacramento St., 415-929-8019
- **Victorian House**, 2318 Fillmore St., 415-923-3237

SPORTING GOODS

Californians are an outdoor bunch, thanks to the fact that the Golden State has deserts, beaches, mountains, hiking, biking and running trails, downhill and cross-country skiing, camping and backpacking opportunities galore, and much, much more. As you might expect, there is no shortage of merchants standing by ready to cater to your every sporting whim. Those listed below are in San Francisco unless otherwise noted.

- **Big 5**, 2159 Chestnut St., 415-474-8620
  314 Gellert Blvd.,Daly City, 415-994-3688
- **Copeland Sports,** Stonestown Galleria, 415-566-5521
- **Don Sherwood Golf and Tennis,** 320 Grant Ave., 415-989-5000
- **Oshman's**, Tanforan Mall, San Bruno, 415-588-0741
- **Play It Again** , 45 W. Portal Ave., 415-753-3049
- **REI**, 1338 San Pablo Ave., Berkeley, 510-527-4140
  1119 Industrial Rd., San Carlos, 415-508-2330
- **SportMart**, 3839 Emery, Emeryville, 510-450-9400
  301 Gellert Blvd., Daly City, 415-301-9000
- **Sunset Soccer**, 2101 Taraval St., 415-664-6888
- **Swiss Ski Sports**, 559 Clay St., 415-434-0322
- **Tennis Shack**, 3375 Sacramento St., 415-928-2255
- **Wise Surfboards**, 3149 Vicente St., 415-665-7745

ALRIGHT, ALRIGHT ... the earth shifts here every once in awhile ... but should you worry about earthquakes? Unfortunately, yes. But whether you should let the probability of seismic activity keep you from living here is questionable. Where on earth can you be totally safe? The flood-country of Johnstown, Pennsylvania? Hurricane-prone Miami or Galveston? Tornado-torn Kansas? Semi-arctic Minnesota? Sweltering Chicago? Each of those areas has experienced painful visits from Mother Nature in the recent past and will probably be visited again in the not too distant future. San Francisco has been victimized by major earthquakes twice — only twice — in nearly 100 years, 1906 and 1989. Granted, the 8.3 magnitude 1906 quake toppled buildings and sparked fires that destroyed much of the city, killing 700 people. The 1989 7.1 magnitude Loma Prieta temblor killed 67, brought down a section of a major East Bay freeway, dislodged part of the Oakland-San Francisco Bay Bridge, sparked fires in the Marina district, and brought the World Series to an abrupt, albeit temporary, halt. But it's only happened twice in nearly a century. So, you'll have to decide if the risk is too great. Rest assured, the San Francisco Bay Area will be hit with more earthquakes. Many speak of the "Big One" that earthquake experts concede will come, although no one will hazard a guess as to when. Six million people live in the Bay Area today, and with all the public awareness programs underway one must assume that most of them know they are living in Quake Country, by choice. Certainly no place on earth is perfect, but, on balance, the San Francisco Bay Area may be as close as one can get.

DISASTER KITS

The secret to surviving a major earthquake seems to be found in the time-proven Boy Scout adage "Be Prepared." There are dozens of good books on the market about how to ready oneself for a seismic onslaught, and plenty of free information available from local, state and federal agencies. They all tell you that you need to be ready to be on your own for three to seven days. It may take that long for emergency crews to restore power, water and telephone service to affected areas. You should also have at least a basic disaster kit prepared, and stored away from areas likely to be damaged in a big earthquake. It should include the following.

- **Food** for each family member *and* your pets (canned goods such as stews, beans, soups, evaporated milk, cereals, granola bars and nuts)
- **Non-electric can opener**
- **Water** (at least three gallons per person per day)
- **Flashlights and extra batteries**
- **Portable radio and extra batteries**
- **Blankets/sleeping bags/pillows**
- **Camping stove and appropriate fuel**
- **Swiss Army knife** or similar tool
- **Cooking and eating utensils, paper plates and cups**
- **Proper sized tent**
- **Water purification tablets**
- **Small bottle of chlorine bleach**
- **Toiletries**, including toilet paper and feminine hygiene products
- **Waterproof matches**
- **First Aid kit**, including the following:
    - plastic adhesive strips
    - ACE bandages
    - gauze pads and tape
    - scissors
    - tweezers
    - safety pins
    - chemical ice packs
    - cotton balls or swabs
    - aspirin or the equivalent
    - antibiotic ointments
    - hydrogen peroxide
    - rubbing alcohol
    - insect repellent
    - thermometer
- **Prescription medications** that are not past their expiration dates
- **Cash** (bank ATMs may not work after a big tremblor and merchants may not be accepting credit cards!)

Once you've gathered everything together put it all in a container, such as a big plastic garbage can with a lid, and stash it in a place that's not likely to be buried in a quake. If you're living in a house, the backyard may be best. If you're living in an apartment building you'll have to be creative when it comes to protecting your investment.

Several Bay Area stores sell earthquake/disaster preparedness equipment and information. Each of them sells earthquake kits as well as the individual components for making one up yourself. This can be a costly endeavor, but when you consider it could be all you have to live on for days following a major earthquake it is certainly worth the expense. Here are just a few of the stores specializing in quake supplies.

- **Earthquake Outlet Supplies,** Ghiradelli Square, San Francisco 415-674-9091
- **Earthquake Outlet**, 2225 Broadway, Redwood City, 415-368-8800
- **Earthquake Outlet,** 981 San Pablo Ave., Albany, 510-526-3587
- **Earthquake Preparedness Associates**, 1163 Francisco Blvd., San Rafael, 415-459-5500

As you put your quake kit together you should also come up with a family emergency plan, in case the earthquake hits when you're not all together in the same place. You can do the same thing with your apartment building neighbors, even if they're not family. Emergency preparedness experts say you should:

- Agree on someone out of the area you can all call to check in, for example, Aunt Mildred in Omaha. She'll want to know how you are as well, so let her be the clearing house for family information. Make sure each family member knows the number and how to dial it. The only chink in this armor is that phone service may not be available for a few days—keep trying, it will eventually be restored.

- Agree on a local gathering place, such as the local high school football field or a department store parking lot; someplace that is not likely to come tumbling down during the initial quake or any aftershocks. Then, make sure everyone understands that that's where they should go if they get home and it's no longer standing.

If you're inside when the earth shifts, remember these three words, *duck, cover and hold.* That means get down, get under something sturdy such as a table or desk, and stay there until the shaking stops. Get away from windows and mirrors and anything else that could tumble down on you.

There are a number of simple steps you can take prior to an earthquake that will make your home a bit safer. They include fastening computers, televisions and other big pieces of equipment to desks and counters so that they won't fall off during the quake. Large furniture items, such as bookcases, should be fastened to the wall. Small items, such as fragile collectibles, should be taped or glued to their shelves. The folks in the earthquake supply stores will be more than happy to sell you what you need to do this or go to a big hardware/home supply store and get the equivalent. Chances are it will be less expensive at the latter. You should also know where the natural gas shutoff valve is located and how to turn it off. This is one of the first things you should check following the earthquake, but turn it off only if you detect a leak. Quake-prepared residents leave the appropriate tool for shutting off the gas valve right next to it at all times. Remember, don't turn the gas off if you don't think it's leaking. The gas company will no doubt be very busy fixing numerous emergency problems following the earthquake so it may be days before someone can get to those who shut things off unnecessarily.

Other Earthquake Information Sources

- **California Seismic Safety Commission** publishes *The Homeowner's Guide to Earthquake Safety* as well as other materials on quake preparedness. 1900 K St., Sacramento, CA 95814. Call 916-322-4917.
- **The Earthquake Preparedness Project** provides pamphlets and other materials on getting ready for a quake. Located at 101 8th St., Oakland, CA 94607. Call 510-540-2713.
- **U.S. Geological Survey**: These folks help to determine the size of the quakes and they are a bottomless pit of information on things seismic. 345 Middlefield Rd., Menlo Park, CA 94025. Call 415-329-4390.

OTHER QUAKE-RELATED NOTES

If you're buying a home in California the seller is required by law to tell you if the property is in the vicinity of an earthquake fault line. Before buying you may want to engage the services of a civil engineer to give your prospective home the once-over, just to make sure it's as safe as it can be. Rental property owners are not required to disclose information about nearby faults to prospective tenants.

Property owners are strongly advised to buy homeowner's insurance. Renters are urged to buy renter's insurance. Both should also get earthquake insurance. The California Insurance Commissioner requires that companies that sell homeowners and renters policies also offer earthquake insurance, so many insurers are no longer writing any new policies in California. That means you may have trouble finding available coverage, but it is out there and a near must-buy. See the "Apartment Hunting" chapter for more information on insurance.

FOR PARENTS coming to the Bay Area you'll be reassured to know that there are many a daycare/babysitting option available. If you just need an occasional babysitter many suggest asking others in similar situations to recommend good sitters they've used. Handle this delicately though, as many people are reluctant to share a reliable babysitter's name for fear that they will lose that sitter to a higher bidder. Local high school counselors and many churches and community centers are also good sources for locating qualified baby-sitters. Depending upon the age and qualifications of the babysitter, hourly rates range from $6 an hour up to $15. You can expect to pay more, and rightly so, for babysitters who have CPR and First Aid training. More and more babysitters have such knowledge and it's worth the added expense to know that they'll be able to handle emergencies while you're away.

If more regular childcare services are required, for example, while you're at work five days a week, your options consist of family-based childcare, in-home care, nannies/*au pairs* or daycare centers.

Family based child care

A licensed provider cares for children in his/her home on a regular basis with other children of like age.

Advantages
- Governed by rules and regulations of state licensing agency, Community Care Licensing
- Checked at least yearly by state licensing officials for compliance with rules and regulations
- Individualized care
- Often flexible hours, including overnights and emergencies
- Inexpensive relative to other options; current Bay Area average: $600 a month.

Disadvantages
- Provider turnover is often high as they tend to close down when their own children begin school
- Often don't work over summer vacation or holidays

In-home child care

A care provider who comes to your home

Advantages
- Kids secure in their own environment and schedules
- Less exposure to disease-causing agents
- Nothing for parents to pack up every day
- Caregiver can often take on other duties such as housekeeping, meal preparation, and shuttle service

Disadvantages
- Usually more expensive than family-based daycare, current Bay Area average is $1000-1400 per month
- What to do if the caregiver can't come for whatever reason?
- Supervision of quality of care lacking, young children often unable to verbalize problems
- Tax responsibilities for parent/employer (although after all the scandals in Washington, there is a good chance that Congress will make tax reporting easier for parent/employers)

Nannies/*Au Pairs*

Short or long-term, often live-in caregivers with special training or qualifications

Advantages
- Similar to those of in-home caregivers
- Cultural enhancement to the family, especially in the case of *au pairs,* who are usually from other countries and come for a year; employer is expected to provide room and board, spending money and airfare; current Bay Area monthly cost average is $800; hired through agencies.
- Nannies hired through agencies are usually trained and screened

Disadvantages
- *Au pairs* only around for a year, creating the possibility of separation anxiety for young children; cost of airfare could be prohibitive for some
- Nannies expensive, current Bay Area average $1000-1400, plus room and board
- Nanny agencies can charge fee of $500-2500.

Daycare Centers

Highly organized, licensed and, in some cases, accredited facilities which provide varying degrees of structure and instruction

Advantages
- Constant supervision and attention to safety issues
- Security; center will probably be around for a while, even following staff changes

• Staff often trained in childhood development

Disadvantages
• Openings can be difficult to find
• Relatively expensive because of high cost of adequate staffing; Bay Area average currently $800 a month
• Center's timetable for daily activities can be at odds with that of the child or parent's routine

No matter which option you choose, there are basic questions that should be asked of any potential care provider.

• Is the caregiver/facility licensed and/or accredited?
• Is the caregiver trained in CPR/First Aid?
• Ask for references/referrals/employment histories and check them out.
• What is the client/employee turnover rate? If it's high, why?
• Is emergency drop-in care available?
• What are holiday/vacation policies?
• What are parental responsibilities in terms of involvement with day-care center or preschool? Is it a co-op?
• Is there an open door policy? May the parent drop in unannounced to observe? (This is, by the way, your legal right. If they are uncom-fortable with this, just walk away and look elsewhere.)
• What is the criteria for hiring staff?
• Are staff backgrounds checked and verified?

For a list of day care centers in the area accredited by the **National Association for the Education of Young Children (NAEYC)** contact the organization at 1509 16th St., Washington D.C. The phone number is 202-232-8777.

To explore the possibility of hiring an *au pair* contact;

• **EF Au Pair,** 800-333-6056
• **Au Pair Homestay,** 800-479-0907
• **Au Pair in America,** 800-928-7247

Bay Area Nanny agencies;

• **Bay Area 2nd Mom,** 415-858-2469
• **I Love My Nanny,** 408-99-NANNY
• **Mothers In Deed,** 415-461-7755 (North Bay)
  415-326-8570 (SF/Peninsula)
• **My Favorite Nanny,** 415-938-3764
• **Nannies Unlimited,** 510-803-1040
• **Town & Country Nannies,** 415-325-2082 (Peninsula/South Bay)
  415-567-0956 (SF/North & East Bay)

CHILD CARE RESOURCES

- **Bananas**, East Bay information, support and referral, 510-658-0381
- **California Childcare Resource & Referral Network**, provides referral and other information statewide for neighborhood by neighborhood childcare options. 111 New Montgomery Street, 7th floor, San Francisco, 94105, 415-882-0234.
- **Children's Council of San Francisco**, childcare referrals and more, 415-243-0111.
- **Family Daycare Information Center,** 800-884-1980
- **Kid Care,** 800-575-4371
- **Marin Childcare Council,** 415-479-2273
- **State Department of Social Services Community Care Licensing**: inspects and licenses daycare homes and centers. San Francisco/Peninsula, 415-266-8843
  South Bay, 408-277-1286
  East Bay, 510-450-3984

PARENTING PUBLICATIONS

- **Bay Area Baby,** 401 Alberto Way, #A, 408-358-7839
- **Bay Area Parent,** Los Gatos 95032, 408-358-1414
- **Parents Press,** 1454 Sixth Street, 800-994-KIDS
  Berkeley 94710 (URL: http://www.family.com)

GRADE SCHOOLS & HIGH SCHOOLS

PUBLIC SCHOOLS IN CALIFORNIA are, in general, struggling to cope with dwindling resources, large classes, and caring but frustrated teachers. Voters approved Proposition 13 a couple of decades ago, an action that drastically reduced education funding. The consequences of that action are being felt today in all public school grades, including those in San Francisco. Thus, according to the California Department of Education, in 1995 California ranked just 35th in the nation in terms of high school SAT scores. The state lottery does funnel millions of dollars into schools now, but a great deal more is needed to pull the system back from the brink. Much hope is being placed on corporate involvement. The good news is that school officials throughout the state seem to know what the problems are and do not seem to be ignoring them.

To find out more about public schools in San Francisco contact the **San Francisco Public Schools** office at 135 Van Ness Avenue. The phone number is 415-241-6000.

You may also want to get in touch with *School Match*, in Westerville, Ohio, to request its report on San Francisco schools. The three-page report will include information on student-teacher ratios, test scores and even property values in your chosen neighborhood. The report will cost $19. *School Match*'s number is 800-992-5323.

COLLEGES & UNIVERSITIES

San Francisco

- **Golden Gate University**: private, non-profit, and accredited, located in the downtown area, GGU offers a wide variety of degree programs in business, law, and public administration. 536 Mission St., call 415-442-7000.
- **San Francisco State University**: part of the California State University system, SFSU offers a wide range of undergraduate and

graduate degrees. Serving more than thirty-thousand students a year, SFSU is one of the largest schools in the CSU system. Located at 1600 Holloway Ave., call 415-338-1111.

- **University of San Francisco**: founded in 1855 by Jesuit fathers, USF was San Francisco's first institution of higher learning. It is fully accredited and beautifully situated on a 50-acre hilltop. USF offers undergraduate and graduate degrees in nursing, business, education, law, and many other disciplines. Located at Parker and Fulton Streets, call 415-666-6762.

East Bay

- **California State University, Hayward**: situated on a hilltop overlooking the city of Hayward to the west, CSU Hayward is a small but respected operation, known locally for its math and education departments. The school offers a wide variety of undergraduate and graduate degree programs. Located at 25800 Carlos Bee Blvd., Hayward, call 510-885-3000.
- **John F. Kennedy University**: founded in 1964, JFK's course offerings are geared toward the adult student looking for a BA and/or MA degree, in fields such as counseling, library or museum arts, management, law and liberal arts. Located at 12 Altarinda Rd., Orinda, call 510-252-0200.
- **Mills College**: founded in 1852, this is the oldest women's college in the western United States. Mills has a long history of excellence in the fields of liberal arts and science. The college offers women undergraduate and graduate degrees, and admits men to some graduate programs. Located at 5000 MacArthur Blvd., Oakland, call 510-430-2255.
- **Saint Mary's College**: located in the hilly, wooded, somewhat secluded community of Moraga, St. Mary's was founded in 1863 by the Christian Brothers. Classes are small, instruction is excellent. Undergraduate and graduate degrees offered. You can find Saint Mary's at 1928 St. Mary's Rd., Moraga, call 510-631-4000.
- **University of California, Berkeley**: considered by many to be the finest school in the UC system, "Cal" has been around since 1868. Located on a 1500 acre wooded urban campus, UCB boasts top notch facilities, faculty, and course offerings in hundreds of disciplines, undergraduate and graduate. Entrance competition is stiff, to say the least. Berkeley, call 510-642-6000.

Peninsula/South Bay

- **San Jose State University**: located in the heart of Silicon Valley in downtown San Jose, SJSU offers some unique opportunities including the use of the nation's only undergraduate nuclear science lab, its own deep-sea research ship, and centers for the study of Beethoven and John Steinbeck. Graduate programs also offered. You can find SJSU at One Washington Square, San Jose, call 408-924-2000.

- **Santa Clara University**: considered by many to be one of the finest universities in the country, Santa Clara is also recognized as California's oldest institution of higher learning. It was founded in 1851 by the Jesuits, in what was to become Silicon Valley. Known for its law, business and engineering schools. Located at 500 El Camino Real, Santa Clara, call 408-554-4000.
- **Stanford University**: certainly one of the nation's premier universities, Stanford is located in comfortable Palo Alto, at the northern end of Silicon Valley. Stanford is known for its excellence in the arts and sciences, its highly-regarded faculty and facilities, including Stanford Medical Center. Established in 1885 by former California Governor and Senator Leland Stanford and his wife Jane. Call 415-723-2300 for information.

North Bay

- **Dominican College**: affiliated with the Catholic Church, Dominican is known for its counseling psychology, education and music programs. Bachelors and Masters degrees are offered. Located at 1520 Grand Avenue, San Rafael, call 415-457-4440.
- **Sonoma State University**: founded in 1960, this is one of the youngest universities in the California State University system. Located 50 miles north of San Francisco, the 220 acre campus east of Rohnert Park reminds many of a park. Degrees and certificates offered in a wide variety of disciplines. Located at 1801 East Cotati Ave., Rohnert Park, call 707-664-2880.

Surrounding Areas

- **University of California, Davis**: located about 70 miles north-east of San Francisco and 15 miles west of Sacramento, UCD is a top-notch research university offering undergraduate and graduate degrees in a wide range of fields. The city of Davis is a beautiful college town, and certainly one of the most bicycle-friendly communities in the nation. Undergraduate admission information is available at 175 Mrack Hall, UCD, Davis. Graduate admission information is available at 252 Mrack Hall, UCD, Davis, call 916-752-1011.

S AN FRANCISCO'S religious community is as diverse as the city's overall population, and there are literally hundreds of houses of worship from which to choose. Every major denomination is represented here along with dozens of lesser-known but certainly no less sincere religious organizations. Here is a representative sampling of houses of worship within the San Francisco city limits. All phone numbers are area code 415.

Advent Christian

- **Parkside Community Church**, Ulloa and 24th Ave., 566-1930

African-American Methodist Episcopal

- **Allen Chapel,** 195 Scotia St., 468-8406
- **Bethel AME**, 970 Laguna St., 921-4935
- **First AME Zion**, 2159 Golden Gate Ave., 931-7479

Apostolic

- **Apostolic Church of the Faith in Christ Jesus**, 100 Felton, 468-1652
- **Apostolic Faith Church**, 1227 Sutter St., 885-6624
- **Calgary Apostolic Church**, 1869 Oakdale Ave., 642-1234

Armenian

- **St. Gregory**, 51 Commonweath Ave., 751-4140
- **St. John's Etchmiadzin**, 275 Olympia Way, 661-1142
- **Calvary Armenian Congregational**, 725 Brotherhood Way, 586-2000

Assemblies of God

- **Ark Ministries**, 3410 19th Ave., 487-0188
- **Bethel Christian**, 1325 Valencia St., 285-1433
- **Community Assembly of God**, 355 Ocean Ave., 584-5250

- **Glad Tidings Temple**, 1475 Ellis St., 346-1111
- **Sunset Bible Assembly**, 1690 21st Ave., 564-3040

Baha'i

- **Baha'i Faith**, 170 Valencia St., 431-9990

Baptist

- **Balboa Baptist**, 200 Onondaga Ave., 585-3778
- **Community Baptist**, 1642 Broderick St., 567-3248
- **Dolores Street Baptist**, 938 Valencia St., 826-2641
- **Ebenezer Baptist**, 275 Divisadero St., 431-0200
- **First Baptist**, 21 Octavia St., 863-3382
- **First Friendship Institutional**, 501 Steiner St., 431-4775
- **Mt. Zion**, 1321 Oak St., 863-4109
- **Paradise Baptist**, 2595 San Jose Ave., 333-0427
- **Park Presidio Bible**, 856 Cabrillo St., 386-7600
- **Star of Hope Missionary**, 2002 Quesada Ave., 282-2810
- **Temple Baptist**, 3355 19th Ave., 566-4080

Bible

- **Park Presidio**, 856 Cabrillo St., 386-7600
- **Sunset Bible Academy**, 1690 21st Ave., 654-3040

Brethren

- **Church of the Brethren Community**, 1811 34th Ave. 681-1025

Buddhist

- **Buddha's Universal**, 720 Washington St., 982-6116
- **Buddhist Assn. of San Francisco**, 5230 Fulton St., 387-6516
- **Dharmadhatu**, 1630 Taraval St., 731-4426
- **Shinnyoen**, 1400 Jefferson St., 346-0209
- **Wong Tai Sin Temple**, 586 6th Ave., 750-9051
- **Zen Center**, 300 Page St., 626-3697

Catholic

- **Cathedral of St. Mary**, 1111 Gough St., 567-2020
- **Dignity San Francisco** (Gay & Lesbian), 1329 7th Ave., 681-2491
- **Mission Dolores**, 3321 16th St., 621-8203
- **Notre Dame Des Victoires**, 566 Bush St., 397-0113
- **Old St. Mary's**, 660 California St., 288-3800
- **St. Agnes**, 1025 Masonic Ave., 487-8560
- **St. Anne of the Sunset**, 850 Judah St., 665-1600
- **St. Cecilia**, 2555 17th Ave., 664-8481
- **St. Dominic's**, Bush and Steiner Streets, 567-7821
- **St. Gabriel Church**, 2559 40th Ave., 731-6161

- **St. Ignatius**, 650 Parker St., 666-0123
- **Star of the Sea**, 4420 Geary Blvd., 751-0450

Charismatic

- **Community Assembly of God**, 355 Ocean Ave., 584-5250
- **Cornerstone Family Fellowship**, 3459 17th St., 861-2439
- **Open Bible Church**, 2135 Market St., 621-3325
- **Voice of the Pentecost**, 1970 Ocean Ave., 333-1970

Christian

- **First Christian**, 599 Duboce Ave., 621-9207
- **Home of Christ**, 465 W. Portal Ave., 564-2099
- **SF Swatow Christian**, 4508 Irving St., 731-8778

Christian Methodist Episcopal

- **Missionary Temple**, 1455 Golden Gate Ave., 921-3324
- **SF Neighborhood**, 302 Jules Ave., 585-2861

Christian Science

- **1st Church**, 1700 Franklin St., 673-3544
- **2nd Church**, 655 Dolores St., 647-0521
- **3rd Church**, 1250 Haight St., 621-2615
- **4th Church**, 300 Funston St., 221-5811
- **5th Church**, 450 O'Farrell St., 474-2747
- **9th Church**, 220 W. Portal Ave., 664-2456

Church of Christ

- **Civic Center**, 250 Van Ness Ave., 861-5292
- **Columbia Heights**, 142 Plymouth Ave., 334-4640
- **Golden Gate**, 8th Avenue and Cabrillo St., 221-2631
- **Lake Merced**, 777 Brotherhood Way, 333-5959

Church of God

- **Church of the Living God**, 740 Clayton St., 753-5799

Church of God in Christ

- **Greater Good Shepherd**, 1633 Ocean Ave., 586-6644
- **Hamilton Memorial**, 2398 Geary Blvd., 346-6864
- **Love Chapel**, 2693 Sutter St., 567-0112
- **St. Beulah**, 435 Duboce Ave., 621-4088

Church of Jesus Christ of Latter-Day Saints

- **San Francisco Stake**, Pacific Ave. and Gough St., 474-6290
- **Sunset Building**, 22nd Ave. and Lawton St., 664-0843

Community

• **Miraloma**, 480 Teresita Blvd., 584-0360

Congregational

• **First Congregational**, Post and Mason Streets, 392-7461

Covenant

• **1st Covenant**, 455 Dolores St., 431-8755

Ecumenical

• **Northern California Ecumenical Council**, 942 Market St., 434-0670

Episcopal

• **All Saints**, 1350 Waller St., 621-1862
• **Church of St. Gregory**, Gough and Bush St., 885-2995
• **Church of the Incarnation**, 1750 29th Ave., 564-2324
• **Episcopal Diocese of California**, 1055 Taylor St., 673-5015
• **Grace Cathedral**, Taylor and California St., 776-6611
• **Holy Innocents**, 455 Fair Oaks St., 824-5742
• **St. Thomas**, 2725 Sacramento St., 928-4601
• **St. Francis**, 399 San Fernando Way, 334-1590
• **St. Luke's**, Van Ness and Clay St., 673-7327
• **Trinity**, 1668 Bush St., 775-1117

Evangelical

• **San Francisco Evangelical Free**, 756 Union St., 391-0699

Free Methodist

• **Free Methodist**, 3811 Mission St., 647-1849

Friends

• **San Francisco Friends-Quaker**, 659th Ave., 431-7440

Gospel of Christ

• **Voice of Christ**, 680 Guerrero St., 626-5890

Greek Orthodox

See Orthodox Eastern

Independent Bible

• **San Francisco Bible**, 498 Funston Ave., 387-3630

Interdenominational

- **Alpha Omega Fellowship**, 1265 Shafter St., 822-3731
- **Church of the Open Door**, 385 Ashton Ave., 586-9625
- **Cornerstone Family Fellowship**, 3459 17th St., 861-2439
- **Ft. Mason Chapel**, Ft. Mason, 928-2619

Jewish (Conservative)

- **Congregation Beth Israel-Judea**, 625 Brotherhood Way, 586-8833
- **Congregation B'Nai Emunah**, 3595 Taraval St., 664-7373
- **Congregation Ner Tamid**, 1250 Quintara St., 661-3383
- **Congregation Sherith Israel**, 2266 California St., 346-1720

Jewish (Orthodox)

- **Adeth Israel,** 1851 Noriega St., 564-5665
- **Congregation Keneseth Israel**, 655 Sutter St., 771-3420
- **Richmond Torah Center of Chabad**, 5138 Geary Blvd., 668-1647

Jewish (Reform)

- **Congregation Emanu-el**, 2 Lake St., 751-2535
- **Congregation Sherith Israel**, 2266 California St., 346-1720

Jehovah's Witness

- **Central Congregation**, 501 Fulton St., 252-7026
- **Golden Gate Park Congregation**, 2500 Fulton St., 752-1919
- **North Beach Congregation**, 1414 Hyde St., 776-4310
- **Portola Congregation**, 220 Campbell Ave., 467-1351
- **Sunset Congregation**, 1666 46th Ave., 566-1500

Lutheran

- **Christ Church ELCA**, 20th Ave. and Quintara St., 664-0915
- **1st Lutheran ELCA**, 6555 Geary Blvd., 751-8108
- **Golden Gate ELCA**, 601 Dolores St., 647-5050
- **Grace LCMS**, 465 Woolsey St., 468-2937
- **Church of the Holy Spirit LCMS**, 3830 Noriega St., 664-4500
- **St. Francis ELCA**, 152 Church St., 621-2635
- **St. Matthew's**, 3281 16th St., 863-6371
- **West Portal Lutheran LCMS**, 200 Sloat Blvd., 661-0242
- **Zion LCMS**, 495 9th Ave., 221-7500

Mennonite

- **Mennonite Church of San Francisco**, 601 Dolores St., 695-2812

Metropolitan

- **Golden Gate Community**, 1600 Clay St., 567-9080
- **Metropolitan Community** (Gay & Lesbian), 150 Eureka St., 863-4434

Muslim

- **San Francisco Muslim Community Center**, 850 Divisadero St., 563-9397

Nazarene

- **Chinese Church of the Nazarene**, 912 Greenwich St., 885-6292
- **Golden Gate Community**, 45 Franklin St., 522-0200
- **Russian Ministry**, 430 29th Ave., 751-3935

New Age

- **Johrei Center**, 1322 Portola Drive, 566-2034
- **New Age Christian Priesthood**, 2940 16th St., 431-8790

Non-denominational

- **Church of the Fellowship**, 2041 Larkin St., 776-4910
- **Church of Amron**, 2254 Van Ness Ave., 775-0227
- **The Church**, 4114 Judah St., 753-9766

Orthodox-Eastern

- **Cathedral of Annunciation**, 245 Valencia St., 864-8000
- **Holy Trinity Cathedral**, 1520 Green St., 673-8565
- **Holy Trinity Greek**, 999 Brotherhood Way, 584-4747
- **Russian Orthodox Church of Our Lady of Kazan**, 5725 California St., 752-2502
- **Nicholas Cathedral**, 2005 15th St., 621-1849
- **Ukrainian Orthodox Church**, 345 7th St., 861-4066

Pentecostal

- **Voice of Pentecost**, 1970 Ocean Ave., 333-1970
- **New Testament**, 1234 Valencia St., 647-9177

Presbyterian

- **Grace Fellowship Community**, 3265 16th St., 864-2105
- **Calvary**, Jackson and Fillmore St., 346-3832
- **1st United**, 1740 Sloat Blvd., 759-3700
- **Lakeside**, 201 Eucalyptus Drive, 564-8833
- **Lincoln Park** 417 31st Ave., 751-1140
- **Noe Valley Ministry**, 1021 Sanchez St., 282-2317
- **Ocean Presbyterian**, 32 Ocean Ave., 587-1100
- **Old First**, 1751 Sacramento St., 776-5552
- **St. John's**, Arguello Blvd. and Lake St., 751-1626
- **St. Paul's**, 43rd Ave. and Judah St., 566-7838

Religious Science
- **Institute of Religious Science**, 3255 Balboa St., 387-8022

Reorganized Latter-day Saints
- **Reorganized Latter-day Saints**, 275 Taraval St., 759-9488

Seventh Day Adventist
- **Central**, 2899 California St., 921-9016
- **Philadelphia**, 2520 Bush St., 567-0263

Spiritualist
- **Aquarian Foundation**, 1448 Pine St., 921-3799
- **Golden Gate Spiritualist Church**, 1901 Franklin St., 885-9976

Taoism
- **Tan Yong Taoist Temple,** 410 26th Ave., 386-2028

Unitarian
- **1st Unitarian**, 1187 Franklin St., 776-4580

United Methodist
- **Calvary United**, 19th Ave. and Judah St., 566-3704
- **1st St. John's**, 1600 Clay St., 474-6219
- **Glide Memorial**, 330 Ellis St., 771-6300
- **Grace United**, 2540 Taraval St., 731-3050
- **Hamilton United**, 1525 Waller St., 566-2416
- **Park Presidio**, 4301 Geary Blvd., 751-4438
- **St. Francis**, 43rd Ave. and Judah St., 566-7838
- **Temple**, 19th Ave. and Junipero Serra Blvd., 586-1444

Unity
- **Unity Christ Church**, 2690 Ocean Ave., 566-4122
- **Unity Church of San Francisco**, 2222 Bush St., 474-0440

IF YOU ARE LOOKING for a guaranteed warm welcome to the Bay Area, or you'd just like to give a little to your fellow man and woman, volunteering your services to any of the organizations below could be just the ticket. Service agencies are always in need of help, and most will have no trouble finding something for you to do, whether you're available for an hour here and there or on a more consistent basis. It feels good, too. All phone numbers below are area code 415 unless otherwise noted.

AIDS

- **AIDS Foundation** 863-2437
- **Face to Face** 267-6121
- **Living Waters** 648-6898
- **Operation Concern** 861-4898
- **Project Open Hand** 558-0600
- **Restoration House** 285-2302
- **Shanti Project** 864-2273

ALCOHOL

- **Alcoholics Anonymous** 621-1326
- **Glide Memorial Church** 771-2772
- **Haight Ashbury Free** 487-5634
- **St. Vincent de Paul** 621-6471
- **Women's Gate** 282-8900

ANIMALS

- **SPCA, SF** 554-3000

CHILDREN

- **Big Brothers/Big Sisters** 434-4860
- **Domestic Violence Hotline** 800-540-5433
- **Polly Klaas Foundation** 800-587-4357
- **SF Child Abuse Council** 668-0494
- **Shriner's Hospital** 665-1100

ELDERLY

- **Card & Visitor Association** 209-269-1405
- **Catholic Charities** 281-1200
- **Friendship Line** 752-3778
- **Legal Assistance** 861-4444
- **Meals on Wheels** 920-1111

DISABLED

- **Council for the Blind** 800-221-6359
- **Crisis Line** 800-426-4263
- **Hearing Society** 693-5870
- **Recreation Center forthe Handicapped** 665-4100
- **Rose Resnick Lighthouse for the Blind** 431-1481
- **United Cerebral Palsy Assn.** 627-6939

DISASTER

- **American Red Cross** 202-0600

ENVIRONMENT

- **Nature Conservancy** 777-0487
- **Sierra Club** 776-2211

GAY/LESBIAN

- **GLAAD** (Alliance Against Defamation) 861-4588
- **Gay Youth Talk Line** 863-3636
- **Metropolitan Church** 863-4434
- **Operation Concern** 861-4898

HEALTH

- **American Cancer Society** 394-7100
- **American Heart Assn.** 433-2273
- **Irwin Blood Bank** 567-6400
- **Shriner's Hospital** 665-1100

HUNGER

- **Glide Memorial Church** 441-6501
- **SF Food Bank** 957-1076
- **St. Anthony's Dining Hall** 241-2600
- **Meals on Wheels** 920-1111
- **Project Open Hand** 558-0600
- **St. Vincent de Paul** 626-1515
- **Salvation Army** 861-0755

LEGAL

- ACLU 621-2488
- Asian Law Caucus 391-1655
- Legal Aid 864-8208
- Legal Assistance for Children 863-3762

LITERACY

- Project Read 557-4388

WOMEN

- NOW 861-8880
- Women Against Rape 647-7273

OTHERS

- SF School Volunteers 274-0250
- United Way 772-4300
- Volunteer Center of SF 982-8999

TO SAY THAT you'll have no shortage of things to do or see in the San Francisco Bay Area is an understatement to be sure. It would actually be more accurate to say that you'll have so many choices you may have trouble deciding what to do first. San Francisco boasts a world class symphony and chorus, opera, ballet, and a vibrant live theater scene, with everything from the experimental and off-beat to big, brash Broadway musicals. It's a rare evening in the Bay Area when one of the current stars of the rock/pop music scene is not appearing locally, and San Francisco provides many a venue for those concerts. The South of Market area is the hub of the city's hip-hop, dance and alternative music scene.

Art lovers indulge themselves at major museums in the downtown area and in Golden Gate Park as well as in smaller galleries throughout the city. There are also science museums, two aquariums, a planetarium and a top-notch zoo.

All of the Bay Area's newspapers print entertainment schedules on a regular basis, so you'll have no trouble finding out what's happening. The most comprehensive listing can be found in the *San Francisco Chronicle/Examiner's Sunday Datebook*. The *Chronicle* also publishes a daily *Datebook* section in the morning newspaper. San Francisco's *Bay Guardian* weekly also has extensive listings and excellent movie reviews and it's free. Look for it in streetside racks.

Tickets for most events and performances may be purchased at the venue box offices or by calling **BASS/Ticketmaster** at 510-762-2277. It's always a good idea to get your tickets as far in advance as possible since many shows, concerts, exhibits and events sell out in advance. When calling ahead, have your credit card ready and be prepared to pay service fees (if your sense of thrift won't allow you to pay the often steep service fees, buy your tickets in person at the box office). For discount, same-day tickets to San Francisco theater productions and full price tickets to other selected local events check out the **TIX Bay Area** ticket booth on the east side of Union Square. This is where last minute open seats are sold for half-price, and while your choices are usually limited you can score great bargains. Call TIX at 415-433-7827. Cash only for half-price tickets. VISA and MasterCard accepted for full-price purchases. Also, there are other ticket agencies listed in the Yellow Pages.

MUSIC-SYMPHONIC, OPERA, CHORAL

The **San Francisco Symphony** is one of the county's premier orchestras. The symphony and its **Chorus** have both won Grammy awards and toured much of the world, performing to packed houses and critical acclaim. World renowned conductor Michael Tillson Thomas runs the show, having recently been handed the baton that was wielded for a decade by maestro Herbert Blomstedt. The local musical community is all in a titter about the style and excitement Thomas brings with him from his previous assignment in front of the London Symphony.

When at home the San Francisco Symphony and Chorus perform, separately and in tandem, at their glittering glass, brass and concrete home, the $33 million Louise M. Davies Symphony Hall. Opened in 1980, the structure underwent an acoustic upgrade in 1992. The concert hall and box office are located in the Civic Center area, at 201 Van Ness Ave. Call the ticket office at 415-431-5400. Ticket prices start around $10 . . . after that, the sky's the limit. Concert season runs from September through May.

The **San Francisco Opera** normally holds court at the War Memorial Opera House, which is right across Van Ness Ave. from City Hall, north of Davies Symphony Hall. However, that building is undergoing seismic upgrading until sometime in 1997, so the company currently performs at the nearby Bill Graham Memorial Civic Auditorium, in the Civic Center and at the Orpheum Theatre at 1192 Market St.

This company attracts many of the opera world's biggest stars and is known for its often lavish productions. Tickets can be on the expensive side, with decent seats starting around $40-$50. The curtain comes up on the opera season with a gala event in September and concludes in the spring. Get your tickets in person at the box office at 199 Grove Street or call 415-864-3330.

San Francisco is also home to the highly acclaimed vocal ensemble, **Chanticleer**. This a cappella group of 8-12 men works year-round, traveling all over the world, performing live and making new recordings. The ensemble specializes in so-called "early music," but is also adept at classical choral works, jazz, pop and spirituals. Catch them when they're in town ... you'll probably be amazed by what you hear. To find out more, call the Chanticleer office at 415-896-5866.

San Francisco's own **Kronos Quartet** is perhaps the chamber ensemble equivalent of the aforementioned Chanticleer. Kronos specializes in modern, experimental music, and it travels the globe playing to sold-out audiences. Check newspaper entertainment guides for the few times Kronos is in the Bay Area to play for its adoring local followers. If you like modern chamber music you're sure to become one of Kronos' many fans.

If you'd like to hear some of the professional musicians of the future, the place to go locally is the **San Francisco Conservatory of Music**. The school is located in the city's Sunset district, at 201 Ortega St. at 19th Ave. Frequent concerts are staged here, featuring classical and contemporary solo and ensemble performers. For more information on upcoming events at the conservatory call 415-759-3477.

BALLET

The **San Francisco Ballet** is a small company with a big reputation. It has been displaced from its home at the War Memorial Opera House, by seismic retro-fitting that is expected to be complete sometime in 1997. While the necessary structural work is being done, the company is flitting from site to site, depending upon its needs and what venues are available. The ballet season follows the opera season. For performance and ticket information call 415-703-9400.

THEATER

The San Francisco theater scene is a lively one, and runs the gamut from experimental to mainstream. The theater district is located two blocks west of Union Square on Geary Street, and is home to the Curran and Geary theaters.

The Curran stages musicals such as the immensely successful "Phantom of the Opera" and other Broadway productions, as well as shows being prepared for the trip to New York's Great White Way. The Geary Theater plays host to what many would consider more serious productions, such as works by Shakespeare, Chekhov, Sam Sheppard and the like. The Geary is also home to one of the most respected theater training programs going, the American Conservatory Theatre. Actress Annette Benning attended ACT after graduating from San Francisco State University.

The Golden Gate Theater, in the nearby Tenderloin district, also stages big, splashy musicals. The surrounding streets are a bit on the seedy side, and that puts many people off when it comes to attending shows here. However, there is safety in numbers, so if possible, stick with the crowd when traveling through this area.

Once you leave the theater district, productions take on a less commercial, more experimental hue, and there are many of them from which to choose. Of course, local high schools, colleges and universities also put on shows, as do many local theater groups. Look for listings for all of the above in newspaper entertainment guides, or call the theaters. Here are just a few of them, all in area code 415.

- **Brava**, 2789 24th St., 487-5401
  (women's issues and themes)
- **Club Fugazi**, 678 Green St., 421-4222
  (home of the immensely popular "Beach Blanket Babylon")
- **Curran**, 445 Geary St., 776-1999 (musicals)

- **Geary**, 415 Geary St., 749-2228
  (serious drama)
- **Golden Gate**, 42 Golden Gate Ave., 473-3800
  (musicals)
- **Lorraine Hansberry**, 620 Sutter St., 474-8800
  (known for top-notch African-American drama)
- **Magic**, Fort Mason, Building D, 441-8822
  (experimental)
- **Marines Memorial**, 640 Sutter St., 771-6900
  (varied)
- **Mason Street**, 340 Mason St., 981-0371
- **Orpheum**, 1192 Market St., 474-3800
  (opera, musicals, serious drama)
- **Theater on the Square**, 450 Post St., 433-9500
- **Theatre Rhinoceros**, 2926 16th St., 861-5079
  (gay and lesbian themes)

CONTEMPORARY MUSIC

San Francisco draws star entertainers as well as up-and-comers from all over the world, as it has done for a long time.

If rock and roll, in any one of its current manifestations, is your cup of tea, no doubt the name Bill Graham will be familiar to you. Graham, the prolific concert promoter, died a few years ago when his helicopter hit a cellular phone transmission tower in the North Bay, but his company, Bill Graham Presents (BGP), presses on. Graham is remembered for, among other things, the local concerts he staged at the Fillmore and the Oakland Coliseum, to name just two of his favorite venues.

The Coliseum is still one of the Bay Area's premier outdoor concert sites, and it also has an indoor stage, the Arena, which is currently undergoing a major face-lift for its prime tenant, the NBA's Golden State Warriors. There are a number of other outdoor facilities used for concerts, chief among them the Shoreline Amphitheater in Mountain View and the Concord Pavilion in Concord. Both have covered seating up front close to the stage, and loads of uncovered lawn behind the seats. Bring a blanket, stretch out and listen to the music.

As previously mentioned, San Francisco's SOMA district is the hub of the Bay Area's alternative, hip-hop and dance music scene. Jazz, blues and folk are also well-represented here. Dozens of nightclubs showcase the talents of the artists you may see at the top of the charts tomorrow, and those who do what they do because they love it, with little concern about making it to "the show."

For the latest on who's playing where and when consult the *San Francisco Chronicle's Datebook* section, or the entertainment guides in the *Bay Guardian* or the *SF Weekly* newspapers. You could also telephone the establishment. Here are some of their numbers and locations.

Larger Concert Facilities

- **Concord Pavilion**, 2000 Kirker Pass Rd., Concord, 510-671-3100
- **Cow Palace**, Geneva Ave. & Santos St., Daly City, 415-469-9988
- **Fillmore**, 1805 Geary Blvd., San Francisco, 415-346-6000
- **Oakland Coliseum & Arena**, Hegenberger Rd. and I-880, Oakland 510-639-7700
- **Shoreline Amphitheater**, 1 Ampitheater Pkwy., Mountain View, 415-967-4040
- **Warfield**, 982 Market St., San Francisco, 415-775-7722

Smaller Concert Facilities

- **Great American Music Hall**, 859 O'Farrell St., San Francisco, 415-885-0750
- **Greek Theatre**, UC Berkeley (near football stadium), Berkeley 510-642-9988

Nightclubs, etc.

We offer you a list of places to get you started though this list is by no means comprehensive.

Rock/Hip-Hop/Blues

- **Ashkenaz**, 1317 San Pablo Ave., Berkeley, 510-525-5054
- **Bottom of the Hill**, 1233 17th St., 415-626-4455
- **Club Chameleon**, 853 Valencia St., 415-821-1891
- **Edinburgh Castle**, 950 Geary St., 415-885-4074
- **Fillmore**, 1805 Geary Blvd., 415-346-6000
- **Freight & Salvage**, 1111 Addison St., Berkeley, 510-548-1761
- **Hotel Utah**, 500 4th St., 415-421-8308
- **Jack's**, 1601 Fillmore St., 415-567-3227
- **Johnny Love's**, 1500 Broadway, 415-931-6053
- **Mick's Lounge**, 2513 Van Ness Ave., 415-928-0404
- **Paradise Lounge**, 1501 Folsom St., 415-861-6906
- **Slim's**, 333 11th St., 415-621-3330

Jazz

- **Annabelle's**, 77 4th St., 415-777-1200
- **Cafe du Nord**, 2170 Market St., 415-861-5016
- **Coconut Grove**, 1415 Van Ness Ave., 415-776-1616
- **Elbo Room**, 647 Valencia St., 415-552-7788
- **Kimball's East**, Emeryville Public Market, Emeryville, 510-658-0606
- **Noe Valley Ministry**, 1021 Sanchez St., 415-282-2317
- **Pearl's**, 256 Columbus Ave., 415-291-8255
- **Radio Valencia**, 1199 Valencia St., 415-826-1199
- **Yoshi's**, 6030 Claremont Ave., Oakland, 510-652-2900

Country

- **Biscuits & Blues**, 401 Mason St., 415-292-2583
- **Paradise Lounge**, 1501 Folsom St., 415-861-6906
- **Starry Plough**, 3101 Shattuck Ave., Berkeley, 510-841-2082

World Music/Reggae

- **Ashkenaz**, 1317 San Pablo Ave., Berkeley, 510-525-5054
- **Bahia Cabana**, 1600 Market St.,415-861-4202
- **Club Dread**, 401 6th St., 415-284-6331
- **Gathering Cafe**, 1326 Grant St., 415-433-4247
- **Plough & Stars**, 116 Clement St., 415-751-1122
- **Sol Y Luna**, 475 Sacramento St., 415-296-8696
- **330 Ritch**, 330 Ritch St., 415-522-9558

COMEDY

There's a lot to laugh about in life, and San Francisco provides ample opportunity to do so at any number of comedy clubs. Some cater to the big-names in modern comedy, including local-boys-made-good Robin Williams, Will Durst, Bobby Slayton and female-funnies Ellen DeGeneres, Carrie Snow, Margaret Cho and Marga Gomez. Others offer open-mike opportunities for up-and-coming jokesters. If your funny bone needs tickling here are a few of the places you may want to visit for comic relief.

- **Cobb's**, 2801 Leavenworth St., 415-928-4320
- **Forked Tongue Cantina**, 493 Broadway, 415-541-5024
- **Josie's**, 3583 16th St., 415-861-7933
- **Punch Line**, 444 Battery St., 415-397-7573
- **Roster T. Feathers**, 157 W. El Camino Real, Sunnyvale, 408-736-0921
- **Tommy T's**, 2410 San Ramon Blvd., San Ramon, 510-743-1500

If comedy is your bag you'll want to plan for the *San Francisco Examiner's* Comedy Celebration Day in Golden Gate Park. It's held every July and features dozens of comedians doing their thing for free. Thousands of people come by car, bus, bike, skateboard, in-line skates and on foot to take in the event. Call the *Examiner* for more information at 415-777-2424.

MUSEUMS

Art

San Francisco is blessed with excellent art museums set in beautiful surroundings, most notably the M.H. de Young Memorial Museum and the Asian Art Museum, both in Golden Gate Park, the new San Francisco

Museum of Modern Art at Yerba Buena Gardens and the newly remodeled California Palace of the Legion of Honor in Lincoln Park. Those are the big ones. There are also many smaller art museums and galleries in the city. Here's an overview of some of them.

- **Ansel Adams Center**, a must-see for any serious photographer or amateur photo buff. The center features photographs taken by its name-sake and others, and sports a well-stocked bookstore. Located at 240 4th St., 495-7000.
- **Asian Art Museum**, featuring artwork, ceramics, architectural displays, jade and textiles from China, Korea, India, Tibet, Japan and Southeast Asia. This is the largest museum of its type on the West Coast, and is indicative of the Bay Area's large Asian population. The collection is actually so sizeable (over ten thousand items) that less than a quarter of it can be displayed at any one time. Currently located in Golden Gate Park, in the same building as the de Young Museum, the Asian Art Museum is scheduled to move in 1998, to the Civic Center building recently vacated by the main branch of the public library. That space will allow the museum to display much more of its collection. John F. Kennedy and Tea Garden Drives, 668-8921.
- **California Palace of the Legion of Honor**, a beautiful building, recently reopened following a seismic upgrade, the palace is perched atop a hill in Lincoln Park, it was given to the city in 1924 by the Spreckels family as a monument to the state's war dead. The art collection features European art from the medieval to the 20th century including a cast of Rodin's *The Thinker*, which sits outside the main entrance. Lincoln Park, 863-3330.
- **M.H. de Young Museum,** named for Michael de Young, a former publisher of the *San Francisco Chronicle*, this museum has been located in Golden Gate Park since construction of the park began in 1917. It features American works from Colonial to Modern, as well as African, British, Egyptian, Greek, Roman and Asian items. The museum is also the site of many lectures and gala events. The de Young also has its own cafe, so you can make a day of it without going hungry. John F. Kennedy Drive, Wed. - Sunday, $6 for adults, $3 for seniors and children under 12, 863-3330 or 750-7645.
- **Mexican Museum,** currently crammed into tiny quarters at Fort Mason, officials here are planning to move this large collection of Mexican and Chicano art to new digs at Yerba Buena Gardens sometime in 1998. Until then it will continue to display works by the likes of Diego Rivera and Nahum Zenil in the Fort's Building D. Fort Mason is in the Marina District. Call the museum at 441-0404.
- **San Francisco Museum of Modern Art**, formerly housed in the Veteran's Building on Van Ness Avenue, SFMOMA now has its own home at Yerba Buena Gardens, and it's one of the most exciting buildings in the city. The building was designed by Swiss architect Mario Botta, and its massive cylindrical skylight is a sight to behold.

Exhibits include works by Henri Matisse, Pablo Picasso and Jackson Pollock, to name just three. SFMOMA was the West Coast's first museum dedicated solely to 20th century art. Located at 151 3rd St., 357-4000.

- **African-American Museum**, Ft. Mason, Building C, 441-0640
- **Cartoon Art Museum**, 814 Mission St., 227-8666
- **Center for the Arts**, 701 Mission St., 978-2700
- **Museo Italoamericano**, Ft. Mason, Building C, 673-2200

Science/Zoos

The Bay Area is a major world scientific research center, home to the Lawrence Livermore and Lawrence Berkeley Laboratories, medical research facilities at the University of California San Francisco and Stanford University Medical Center, and, of course, Silicon Valley, where the computer, communications, and medical technologies of the future are being developed. All that, and more, feeds a vibrant science education community, that attempts to inspire and encourage the researchers of tomorrow. Children and adults love to visit the science museums listed below.

- **California Academy of Sciences**, located in a sprawling building in Golden Gate Park, right across the street from the de Young art museum, was founded in 1853 and is the oldest scientific institution in the western United States. The facility includes the **Morrison Planetarium**, and the **Steinhart Aquarium**. One of the aquarium's most popular attractions is the Fish Roundabout that allows you to watch as all manner of shark, bat rays, and schools of fish swim around you in a one hundred thousand gallon tank. There are astounding displays of reptiles and amphibians and some of the most bizarre fish you'll ever see, as well as a varied display of underwater plant-life. Call 750-7145, for information on the Academy and the aquarium. For information on activities at the planetarium call 750-7141.
- **Exploratorium**, located in the Palace of Fine Arts in the Marina district, this is a true "hands on" scientific experience for everyone. There are nearly seven hundred exhibits, many of them interactive, and all highly educational. One of the most popular attractions is the Tactile Dome. Reservations are required for the opportunity to tumble around inside this darkened dome, where you rely on nothing but touch and sound. Located at 3601 Lyon St., 563-7337.
- **San Francisco Zoo**, this 65-acre facility is perhaps best known for its koalas and Gorilla World. Few zoos have koalas, so they are a real treat to see as they cling, fast asleep, to their habitat's eucalyptus branches. The gorilla display is reportedly one of the world's largest. There's also a Children's Zoo, that allows kids to pet some of the animals, and an Insect Zoo that is sure to give you the creeps. Sloat Blvd. at 45th Ave., 753-7083.

- **Underwater World**, opened in 1996 at the tourist magnet of Pier 39, this attraction takes visitors literally into the aquarium through a long plastic tunnel. All around you the aquarium's residents glide by in an environment that can make you feel as though it is people, rather than fish, that are on display. Pier 39, 623-5300.

History

- **Cable Car Museum**, get a close look at the history and inner workings of the nation's only moving national landmark, San Francisco's world famous cable cars. Located at Washington and Mason Streets, 474-1887.
- **Chinese Historical Society of America**, San Francisco's Chinatown has long been one of the largest Chinese communities in the country, and this small museum is dedicated to its history and that of the people who created it. Located at 650 Commercial St., 391-1188.
- **Jewish Museum**, this modest historical museum doubles as an art museum featuring works by Jewish artists. Located at 121 Steuart St., 543-2090.
- **Communications Museum**, 140 New Montgomery St., 542-0182
- **Maritime Museum**, Fisherman's Wharf, 556-3002
- **Museum of the City of San Francisco**, 2801 Leavenworth St., 928-0289
- **North Beach Museum**, 1435 Stockton St., 626-7070
- **Oakland Zoo**, 580 E. Golf Links Rd., Oakland, 510-632-9525
- **San Francisco Fire Department Museum**, 655 Presidio Ave., 558-3546

MOVIES

Art, Revival, International

Mainstream theaters showing the latest Hollywood blockbusters are located throughout much of the city. They are not hard to find. (Some still offer bargain matinees in the afternoon.) Below is a list of San Francisco's harder-to-find "art houses" which specialize in foreign and/or alternative films.

- **Bridge**, 3010 Geary Blvd., 352-0810
- **Castro**, Castro St. near Market St., 621-6120
- **Clay**, Fillmore St. near Clay St., 352-0810
- **Embarcadero**, 1 Embarcadero Center, 352-0810
- **Four Star**, Clement St. and 23rd Ave., 666-3488
- **Gateway**, 215 Jackson St., 352-0810
- **Lumiere**, California St. near Polk St., 352-0810
- **Opera Plaza**, Van Ness and Golden Gate Avenues, 352-0810
- **Red Vic**, 1727 Haight St., 668-3994
- **Roxie**, 3117 16th St., 863-1087
- **Vogue**, Sacramento St. and Presidio Blvd., 221-8183

FILM FESTIVALS

San Francisco hosts five annual film festivals.

- **San Francisco Asian Film Festival** (March), 863-0814
- **San Francisco International Film Festival** (April), 931-3456
- **International Lesbian & Gay Film Festival** (June), 703-8650
- **Jewish Film Festival** (July), 510-548-0556
- **Festival Cine Latino** (September), 553-8135

COMPUTER ON-LINE SERVICES

There is no shortage here of on-ramps to the information superhighway, whether you want full-service, such as America Online or CompuServe, or basic Internet access. The best place for up-to-date information on all things computer-related is *Computer Currents* magazine. It comes out twice a month and is available at racks along downtown sidewalks. Best of all, it's free. If you already know the service you want to use, but just need the telephone number, here are a few of the big ones serving the Bay Area.

Full Service

- **America Online**, 800-827-6364
- **CompuServe,** 800-848-8199
- **Microsoft (MSN)**, 800-776-3449
- **The Well,** 800-935-5885

Internet Only

- **Slip, Net,** 415-281-4447
- **Hooked,** 800-2HOOKUP
- **West Coast Online,** 800-926-4683
- **Sirius,** 415-284-4700
- **SpryNet**, 800-777-9638

PROFESSIONAL

Bay Area sports fans are blessed (although some might say cursed) with professional teams in all of the major leagues, baseball, basketball, football, hockey and soccer.

Baseball

One of the Bay Area's most intense sports rivalries exists between the National League **San Francisco Giants** and the American League **Oakland Athletics** (the A's). The Giants and the A's wind up the preseason every year by squaring off against each other in the Bay Bridge Series, played at both 3COM Park (otherwise known as Candlestick Park) and the Oakland Coliseum. The last time the A's and Giants met in the World Series was in 1989. That series was disrupted by the October 17th Loma Prieta earthquake that rattled then-Candlestick Park. The A's went on to win the series four games to three.

3COM Park is the current home of the Giants, but the organization is working to raise funds for a new baseball-only facility in the city's China Basin area. 3COM is notoriously windy and cold, even in the summer, when the chilling fog rolls in from the ocean to the west. The Oakland Coliseum is a much nicer ballpark for baseball, and has recently been renovated. Tickets can be purchased at the respective ballpark box offices as well as through any number of ticket agencies. Check the phone book for ticket agency numbers. Here are the box office numbers.

- **San Francisco Giants**, 3COM Park, Jamestown Ave. and Harney Way, San Francisco, 415-467-8000
- **Oakland Athletics**, Oakland Coliseum, I-880 and Hegenberger Rd., Oakland, 510-638-0550

Basketball

The NBA's **Golden State Warriors** normally play their home games in the Oakland Coliseum Complex's Arena, but it's being renovated, in an attempt to keep the organization from permanently leaving town. Until that work is done, sometime in 1997, they'll be tipping off at the San Jose Arena, in downtown San Jose. Tickets can still be purchased at the Coliseum's Warrior Box Office at 510-639-7700, or at many Bay Area ticket agencies. The San Jose Arena is at W. Santa Clara and Autumn Streets and can be reached at 408-287-9200.

Football

Oakland and San Francisco are intense rivals when it comes to football, the former being the home of the **Oakland Raiders**, the latter home to the **San Francisco 49ers**. These teams, two of the most successful franchises in the National Football League, rarely play each other because they are in different conferences, but when they do it's quite a local event. The Raiders play at the Oakland Coliseum (location and box office number listed above under Oakland A's baseball listing). The 49ers play at 3COM Park, (location listed above under San Francisco Giants baseball listing), box office number is 415-468-2249.

Hockey

The Bay Area boasts two professional ice hockey teams, the **San Francisco Spiders**, of the International Hockey League, and the **San Jose Sharks**, of the National Hockey League. Both teams are fairly new franchises. The Sharks have certainly endeared themselves to local hockey fans. They play in the San Jose Arena, affectionately known as the "Shark Tank." The Spiders on the other hand, who have played in the Cow Palace in Daly City, are struggling, and at publication time faced an uncertain future. According to the box office, the Spiders are taking the 1997-98 season off and will no longer be playing at the Cow Palace upon their return. Only time will tell. Tickets for the Sharks are available at numerous Bay Area ticket outlets or at the ticket office at the Arena, 408-287-7070. For information on the future of the Spiders call 415-656-3000.

Horse Racing

There are no race tracks in San Francisco, but there are two within a half an hour's drive of the city. **Golden Gate Fields** is located at 1100 Eastshore Highway, in the East Bay city of Albany. For more information call 510-559-7300. On the Peninsula there's **Bay Meadows**, at 2600 S. Delaware St. in San Mateo, 415-574-7223. Bay Meadows' days may be numbered, however, at least at its current location, as developers are said to be eyeing the property for residential development.

Soccer

1996 brought professional soccer to the Bay Area for the first time in years in the form of Major League Soccer's **San Jose Clash.** The team played its first season at Spartan Stadium on the San Jose State University campus. The team is reportedly working to build its own stadium, perhaps in nearby Santa Clara, but at publication time it was merely a proposal. For Clash ticket information call 408-985-4625.

COLLEGE SPORTS

If you'd like to watch the sports stars of tomorrow in training you may want to follow one or more Bay Area college or university teams.

Perhaps the most closely followed collegiate sports contest in the Bay Area is the annual **Big Game** that pits the University of California Golden Bears against the Stanford Cardinals on the football field. It's usually a spirited event, and a consistent sell-out. Get your tickets early.

The Stanford women's basketball team has been one of the best in the country in recent years, and Cardinal fans are hoping that continues.

Here are just a few of the bigger schools that field teams in a variety of sports and how to find out more information about their programs.

- **Stanford University** plays basketball at Maples Pavilion, football at Stanford Stadium, both located on the university campus in Palo Alto. For information call 415-723-1021.
- **University of California at Berkeley** plays basketball in the Harmon Arena, football at Memorial Stadium, both on the Berkeley campus. For more information call 800-462-3277.

Sporting events are also staged by the following schools:

- **San Francisco State University**, 415-338-2218
- **St. Mary's College**, 510-631-4392
- **Santa Clara University**, 408-554-6921
- **San Jose State University**, 408-824-1200

PARTICIPANT SPORTS AND ACTIVITIES

San Francisco and environs are a haven for sports enthusiasts who love to walk, run, bike, hike, camp, sail, play tennis, baseball, football, soccer, swim, lift weights, do aerobics and any number of other physical activities. Below are just a few of the dozens of pursuits open to you here in the Bay Area.

Bicycling

There are numerous biking trails and bike lanes all around the Bay Area, offering a wide variety of terrain and views. One of the most exciting developments in recent years has been the effort to build a trail ringing the entire bay, giving cyclists and walkers alike the opportunity to circumnavigate the entire area without leaving the same trail. Only portions of the so-called **Bay Trail** have been built to date, but supporters of the project say they have no doubt it will eventually be completed. Some of the best rides in San Francisco are in Golden Gate Park, along the

Embarcadero, and along the Golden Gate Promenade, from the Marina to Ft. Point beneath the south end of the Golden Gate Bridge.

Taking your bike across the bay is also a fairly easy thing to do, thanks to the fact that BART allows bikes during non-commute hours. You must ride in the last BART car, but it's a clean, fast ride. Some bus systems also accommodate bikes, as do the many ferry boats that criss-cross the bay, providing access to the trails and paths of Marin County and the East Bay. Bike riders younger than 18 must wear a helmet, according to California law. Violators are subject to fines.

Boating

Opening Day on the Bay is an annual event that brings out hundreds of sailors on a hopefully sunny day in May. It serves as the ceremonial, if not the official, kickoff of the summer sailing season. If you just want to watch, find a position along the Golden Gate Promenade, which is between the **St. Francis Yacht Club**, at the west end of the Marina, and Ft. Point, which is just beneath the San Francisco end of the Golden Gate Bridge. The St. Francis Yacht Club is seriously backing an effort to bring the America's Cup race to the San Francisco Bay in the not-too-distant future.

If you don't know how to pilot a sailboat, but you'd like to learn, here are a few names and numbers of outfits providing instruction that should put you on the right tack. All are located in area code 415.

- **Day on the Bay**, San Francisco Marina, 922-0227
- **Cass Sailing School**, 1702 Broadway, Sausalito, 332-6789
- **Modern Sailing Academy**, 2310 Marinship Way, Sausalito, 331-8250
- **Spinnaker Sailing**, Pier 40, 543-7333

Bowling

Some might argue that it's not quite a sport ... but few would argue that it's a lot of fun. San Francisco, unfortunately, is woefully under-bowled, particularly with the recent closure of Rock 'n Bowl. Diehard Kegelers can console themselves at the following two alleys:

- **Japantown Bowl**, 1790 Post (at Webster), 921-6200
  Boasts 40 lanes, coffee shop, lounge, satellite TV and, best of all, three free hours of validated parking at the Japan Center Garage across the street.
- **Presidio National Park Bowl**, Building #93 (between the Presidio's Moraga and Montgomery Streets), 561-2695
  Try out the 12 proud lanes where Generals Powell and Schwarzkopf might have bowled when they were in the San Francisco.

Golf Courses

There are many public courses in the Bay Area. The following are in, or are close to, San Francisco.

- **Cypress Golf Course** (9 holes), 2001 Hillside Blvd., Colma, 992-5155
- **Gleneagles International**, 2100 Sunnydale Ave., 587-2425
- **Harding Park**, 99 Harding Rd., 664-4690
- **Presidio**, Presidio National Park, 751-1322

Hiking

If taking off for a day-long hike away from the urban bustle is something that strikes your fancy, you'll have plenty of opportunities to indulge yourself in the Bay Area, without straying too far from home. **Presidio National Park**, in San Francisco, the **Marin Headlands**, just beyond the northern end of the Golden Gate Bridge, and **Tilden Park** in the Oakland/Berkeley hills, are just three of the best known. The **Point Reyes National Seashore**, about 90 minutes north of San Francisco, is also a great spot for hiking, despite a recent wildlands fire there that blackened hundreds of acres.

If you want to escape for more than a day, consider **Yosemite National Park** which is located about 4 hours drive to the east, in the Sierra Nevada. Yosemite is a popular vacation destination for many Bay Area residents. Despite what you may have heard about the crowds in the park, the only consistently crowded part is Yosemite Valley; if you set out on foot for the high country you *can* leave the motorhomes behind.

Skating

Roller skating and in-line skating are both popular activities in San Francisco, especially on weekends in Golden Gate Park. If you don't own your own skates head for Fulton Street along the northern end of the park in the morning and look for the brightly-colored rent-a-skate vans parked there. They'll be happy to fix you up.

If you'd rather skate in a rink, you're out of luck in San Francisco, but San Mateo, about 20 minutes south of the city, has a rink. Check out **Rolladium Roller Rink** at 363 N. Amphlett Blvd., 415-342-2711. If you're looking for an ice skating rink you may want to head for **Belmont Ice Rink**, in Belmont at 815 Old County Rd. or **Berkeley Iceland**, at 2727 Milvia St., in Berkeley. Belmont Ice Rink's phone number is 415-592-0532. Iceland's number is 510-843-8800. A new ice skating rink is being planned for San Francisco's Moscone Convention Center area, but it won't be ready until sometime in 1998.

Skiing

Sierra Nevada ski resorts are three-and-a-half to four-and-a-half hours to the east of the Bay Area, along Interstate 80 and Highway 50. If you don't own your ski gear there are several local businesses that will rent everything you need to hit the slopes or cross-country trails in style, including the well-respected **Recreational Equipment Incorporated (REI)**. Unfortunately REI doesn't have a San Francisco store, but there is one in Berkeley, at 1338 San Pablo Ave., 510-527-4140, and another in San Carlos, at 1119 Industrial Rd., 415-508-2330. Other places to check, **FTC Sports**, at 415-673-8363, and **Swiss Ski Sports**, at 415-434-0322, both in San Francisco. For additional outfitters, try the Yellow Pages.

Swimming

For those few days when it actually gets hot enough to swim in San Francisco the city has kindly provided a selection of public pools. Hours vary, so the best bet is to call ahead. Here are city pool names, locations and phone numbers, all area code 415.

- **Angelo Rossi**, Arguello Blvd. and Anza St., 666- 7011
- **Balboa Park**, Ocean and San Jose Avenues, 337-4715
- **Garfield Pool,** 26th and Harrison Streets, 695-5010
- **Hamilton Rec. Center**, Geary Blvd. and Steiner St., 292-2008
- **North Beach Playground**, Lombard and Mason Streets, 274-0201

Some private clubs have pools including the **Golden Gateway Tennis and Swim Club** (GGTSC), at 370 Drumm St., and the **Bay Club**, at 1 Lombard St. Call the GGTSC at 616-8800 and the Bay Club at 433-2550.

Tennis

There are public tennis courts all over the city, and most of them are first come, first served. Golden Gate Park has 21 courts, at the east end of the park, that may be reserved by calling 753-7100. There are also quite a few private clubs in and around San Francisco. See the listing for the **Golden Gateway Tennis and Swim Club** and **Bay Club** "Swimming" listing above. Another popular location is the appropriately named **San Francisco Tennis Club**, at 645 5th St., 777-9000.

Other Health Clubs

If you're looking for a place downtown at which to work out, you'll have no shortage of options. Here are some of the clubs with locations in the Financial District and surrounding areas, all 415 area code.

- **Bay Club**, 555 California St., 362-7800
  150 Greenwich St., 433-2200
- **Club One,** 1 Sansome St., 399-1010
  360 Pine St., 398-1111
  2 Embarcadero Center, 788-1010
- **Gold's Gym,** 501 2nd St., 777-4653

- **Pinnacle,** 345 Spear St., 495-1939
  61 New Montgomery St., 543-1110
- **Telegraph Hill** 1850 Kearny St., 982-4700
- **24 Hour Nautilus** numerous locations 1-800-24-WORKOUT
- **YMCA**, 169 Steuart St., 957-1940
- **YWCA**, 620 Sutter St., 775-6502

PARKS

Golden Gate Park

The idea to create a large park in San Francisco surfaced in the mid-1860s as city leaders tried to figure out a way to wrest control of a large piece of city land occupied by squatters. Most of what is now the 1,017 acre park (to give you an idea of its size, New York City's Central Park is only 750 acres) was then nothing more than rolling sand dunes.

The method for reclaiming the land, and turning it into the greenspace it is today, was reportedly hit upon by accident, by William Hammond Hall, the park's designer and its first Superintendent. It seems a horse's nosebag full of barley fell to the sand and unexpectedly sprouted. Hall took note of this and decided to plant barley, grass and other plants throughout the sandy areas to be reclaimed, and the rest is history. Hall is credited with keeping traffic moving slowly through the park by insisting that the roads that criss-cross the park be winding ones.

William Hall was the park Superintendent from 1871-1876, but before he left he appointed John McLaren as Assistant Superintendent. McLaren, a native of Edinburgh, Scotland, would become Superintendent in 1890, and went on to make quite a name for himself, as he continued the reclamation process, with the help and advice of horticulturists from around the world. Word is he alone planted about a million trees over his lifetime. After his death in 1943, "Uncle John", as he was lovingly known, was honored by city leaders who named the park's headquarters, and his former home, McLaren Lodge.

Today Golden Gate Park is the city's playground, seven days a week. No matter what the weather, the trails are being used by walkers, joggers, roller-skaters and bike riders. The meadows and groves are popular picnic sites, many of which come with barbecues, and require reservations on weekends. The park also boasts numerous lakes and streams (including one that appears to run uphill), baseball diamonds, soccer fields, tennis courts, playgrounds, an antique carousel, two art museums, a science museum and an aquarium, a Japanese tea garden and much more. Despite all that activity, Golden Gate Park offers many a quiet, secluded spot for those seeking a bit of solitude.

The park spreads out from its eastern border of Stanyan Street to the ocean, three miles to the west. It's about a half mile wide, separating the Richmond district to the north and the Sunset to the south.

For further information or reservations call:

- **Asian Art Museum** 668-8921
- **Baseball/softball diamonds** 753-7024
- **Boating** (Stow Lake) 752-0347
- **California Academy of Sciences** 750-7145
- **M. H. de Young Art Museum** 863-3330
- **Fly casting** (Angler's Lodge) 386-2630
- **Football** (Polo Field) 753-7025
- **Golf** (nine hole course) 751-8987
- **Guided walks** 221-1311
- **Horses** (stables) 668-7360
- **Lawn bowling** 753-9298
- **Picnic/barbecue** 666-7027
- **Soccer** 753-7025
- **Tennis** (21 courts) 753-7100
- **Conservatory of Flowers** 752-8080
- **Tea Garden** 752-1171
- **Strybing Arboretum** 661-1316

Presidio National Park

Founded by the Spanish in 1776, the 1590 acre Presidio had been a military installation until October 1994, when the National Park Service assumed command. Soon after that the U.S. Sixth Army packed up and shipped out for good. The old base boasts some of the Bay Area's prime real estate, more than one hundred miles of roads and wooded trails, ocean vistas, a world class golf course, and two hundred years of military history. The facility served as a training base for Union troops in the Civil War and, in the aftermath of the 1906 earthquake that destroyed much of San Francisco, as a refuge for displaced residents struggling to put their crumbled lives together again. It was also a World War II command center.

The park is located at the northern tip of the San Francisco peninsula, along the southern edge of the Golden Gate, the entrance to the bay. For more information on what the park has to offer call the **Visitor's Center** at 415-561-4323. History buffs may want to check out the **Presidio Army Museum**, at Funston Avenue and Lincoln Blvd., 415-921-8193. If you're interested in teeing off at the **Golf Course** call 415-561-4653. Kegelers can try out the park's 12 lane **Bowling Alley** in Building #93 (between Moraga and Montgomery Streets), call 415-561-2695 for more information.

Other San Francisco Parks

- **Harding Park**, Harding Drive off Skyline Drive, 753-1101
- **McLaren Park**, University & Woolsey Streets, 337-4700
- **Mission Dolores**, Dolores & 19th Streets, 554-9529
- **Balboa Park**, Ocean Ave. & San Jose St., 337-4715
- **Glen Park**, Bosworth St. & O'Shaughnessy, 337-4705
- **Crocker Amazon**, Moscow & Italy Streets, 337-4708

For more information on the **San Francisco Recreation & Parks Department** call 415-666-7200. For information about other **National Parks** in the Bay Area call 415-556-0560.

BEACHES

If you think all of California's beaches are like the ones seen on "Baywatch" think again. Those are Southern California beaches. Northern California beaches are much different than the miles-long ocean-front playgrounds seen on the small screen.

Bay Area beaches are often socked-in by fog in the mornings, and temperatures rarely top the 70s or 80s in the afternoons. Nevertheless, there are a number of popular beaches in San Francisco, including the appropriately named **Ocean Beach**, along the western edge of Golden Gate Park. Hang-gliders and kite-fliers love the beach at **Fort Funston**, south of Ocean Beach. Nudists throw caution to the wind at the beach at **Land's End**, on the northern edge of Lincoln Park. Families flock to **Baker Beach**, which is along the western edge of the Presidio, for the views of the ocean, the Golden Gate Bridge and the Marin Headlands to the north. **China Beach** is a small secluded stretch of sand adjacent to the upscale Sea Cliff neighborhood. Marin county's **Stinson Beach** is perhaps the Bay Area's most popular beach. As a matter of fact it is so popular that on summer weekends you should beware of the thousands of vehicles, and inevitable traffic jams, on Highway 1 along the coast north of San Francisco as city slickers rev up their engines in search of peace and quiet.

There are much quieter beaches along the San Mateo County coastline so if you'd like to avoid the crowds head south from San Francisco down Highway 1, through **Pacifica** and **Half Moon Bay** and keep your eyes peeled for a beach that fits the bill. Remember, though, that the water is cold, and the underwater currents are strong.

ALIFORNIA IS WIDELY KNOWN for its "car culture" and rightly so. Despite the best efforts of alternative transportation advocates, Bay Area freeways clog every weekday morning and afternoon, often to the point of gridlock, even though there are excellent public transit options available. As traffic worsens, more and more Bay Area residents will choose to leave their cars at home, but the battle is still far from won.

TRAINS

BART

The king of local transportation systems is the **Bay Area Rapid Transit** (**BART**), high-speed above- and below-ground trains that whisk travelers through one of the world's longest underwater tunnels between San Francisco and the East Bay, while above ground people inch along in massive traffic jams.

BART currently runs four lines between three dozen stations. It is also expanding service further into the East Bay and hopes to have a station at San Francisco International Airport, which is actually in San Mateo County, by the turn of the century. San Mateo County supervisors voted against taking BART service when the system was just a dream nearly three decades ago, a decision most Peninsula transportation planners now say was a blunder.

Trains currently run weekdays from 4am to 1am, Saturdays 6am to 1am, and Sundays 8am to midnight. Fares are based on distance traveled and range from about $1 to $3.50 one way. BART officials are considering rate hikes to pay for new stations and system upgrades, and chances are they will get what they want, sometime in 1997. Best of all, BART trains are clean, quiet, and usually on time.

BART stations are also connection points for local bus service, so it's fairly easy to get just about anywhere in the Bay Area on public transit. All BART stations are wheelchair accessible. Bicycles are allowed on BART as well, during non-commute hours.

For schedule and fare information, drop by the Customer Service window at the Lake Merritt BART station in Oakland, during normal business hours, or, call 510-464-6000. TDD/TTY access is available for the hearing impaired at 510-839-2220.

CalTrain

For Peninsula and South Bay residents who don't have the luxury of BART service (because BART does not extend to either area) the commuter rail option is CalTrain. This service runs between Gilroy in the South Bay and San Francisco's 4th Street Station. Once you get to San Francisco you'll need to take a bus, cab or walk into the Financial District. There's long been talk of extending CalTrain's tracks to the Transbay Terminal at 1st and Mission Streets but nothing has been done yet. Fares are based on distance and tickets can be purchased at any CalTrain station. Trains run Monday through Friday from 4:44am to 10:30 pm. Bikes are allowed.

For more information call 800-660-4287. TDD/TTY service for the hearing impaired at 415-508-6448

Amtrak

Amtrak does not serve San Francisco proper but it does run through the Bay Area, coming into the East Bay from Sacramento, running down to San Jose and beyond. Amtrak trains make stops in Richmond, Emeryville, Oakland and San Jose. The easiest way to get to San Francisco from an East Bay Amtrak stop is to depart the train at the Richmond station and connect there to a BART train headed for the city.

For information call 800-USA-RAIL.

BUSES

San Francisco Municipal Railway (MUNI)

San Francisco's bus system or MUNI employs a variety of vehicles including diesel and electric buses, electric trolleys (some of them vintage), MUNI Metro light-rail-vehicles and the world renowned cable cars. MUNI operates 80 lines, 17 of them express, as well as special service to 3COM Park for San Francisco Giants and 49ers games and other events. In general, service is available 24 hours, although not on all lines. The current adult fare is $1 one way, except on the cable cars which cost $2. Exact change is required on all MUNI vehicles, except for the cable cars. Transfers are available on all MUNI lines, as are discounts for seniors, youths and the disabled, and monthly passes.

For more information on MUNI service call 415-673-MUNI. TDD/TTY service is available at 415-923-6366. Disabled service information available at 415-923-6142.

Alameda-Contra Costa Transit (AC)

This is the bus system that connects the East Bay to San Francisco, serving Alameda and Contra Costa counties. There are commute hour Transbay express routes. AC also connects with all East Bay BART stations.

For more information on AC Transit call 800-559-4636. TDD/TTY service for the hearing impaired at 800-448-9790.

San Mateo County Transit (SamTrans)

SamTrans provides Peninsula residents with local bus service and has routes to downtown San Francisco. It also links San Francisco International Airport to the BART system at its Colma station with its 3X bus. The 3X runs every 20-30 minutes, 7 am-10 pm, seven days a week, making it possible for airline passengers to get to and from the airport entirely on public transit if they have access to a BART station.

For more information on SamTrans call 800-660-4287. TDD/TTY service for the hearing impaired at 415-598-6448.

Golden Gate Transit

Golden Gate Transit or GGT provides local bus service for Marin County communities and commute bus and ferry service between Marin and Sonoma counties and downtown San Francisco. The ferries depart for San Francisco from the Larkspur Ferry Terminal and a Sausalito dock that is just off of Bridgeway, that community's main street. There is plenty of free parking at the Larkspur facility and metered parking close to the Sausalito launch point. There is no more civilized or more relaxing way to commute than on the ferry, and more and more people are choosing to take the boat these days. Note to unattached but seeking: numerous romances have blossomed on this yuppie loveboat. Drinks and snacks are served. The trip across the bay takes about 30 minutes.

For more information on the bus and ferry service call 415-453-2100. TDD/TTY at 415-257-4554.

- **Contra Costa County Connection** provides local bus service in Contra Costa County, call 510-676-7500. TDD/TTY 800-735-2929.
- **Santa Clara County Transit** offers bus and light rail service to the South Bay, call 800-894-9908. TDD/TTY 408-321-2330.
- **Greyhound** has numerous stations throughout the Bay Area, call 415-558-6789.

FERRIES

Alameda-Oakland Ferry

Providing an aquatic link to downtown San Francisco for East Bay residents, this service is similar to Golden Gate ferry service outlined above. Those who use the boat regularly often develop friendships that continue on land and you can be sure there is plenty of professional networking taking place on board. The boats leave, seven days a week, from Oakland's Jack London Square, at the foot of Broadway and from Alameda's Main Street terminal, and docks at San Francisco's Ferry Building and at Fisherman's Wharf. Food and beverage service is available.

For more information call 510-522-3300.

Golden Gate Transit

See listing above under BUSES.

AIRPORTS

San Francisco International Airport

Located 15 miles south of downtown San Francisco, San Francisco International Airport (SFO) sits across Highway 101 and the Peninsula cities of Millbrae and San Bruno. This big daddy of Bay Area airports is currently undergoing a major remodeling and construction effort as a new International Terminal is being built. BART officials would like to extend train service into SFO by 2000. Airport officials warn of increased traffic congestion and full long-term and short-term parking lots due to this construction.

There is no shortage of transportation options between the airport and San Francisco. A taxi or a limo will set you back at least $25. One of the many shuttle vans, such as **SuperShuttle** (415-558-8500), will cost about $10, but you may have to sit through a number of stops before you get to your destination. If you've got time to kill, and you'd really like to save cash, catch the 3X SamTrans bus outside the International or United Terminals. The 3X will take you straight to the Colma BART station for about $1. Then take BART into the city for about $2 more. (For more on the 3X see the SamTrans entry above, under BUSES.)

For more information on SFO call 415-761-0800. For SFO parking information call 415-877-0227 (24 hours).

Oakland International Airport

This East Bay airport is easier to use than San Francisco International for one simple reason: it is much smaller than its southern Goliath. While SFO is serviced by many major U.S. and international carriers, Oakland Airport focuses on commuter and low cost airlines, such as Southwest and the United Shuttle. Oakland Airport is fairly easy to get into and out of by car, and is also served on a regular basis by a shuttle from BART's Coliseum station. Parking is usually available at Oakland Airport, even during peak holiday travel periods. The airport is located at the west end of Hegenberger Road, a clearly-marked exit from Interstate 880.

For general information on Oakland Airport call 510-577-4000. For the latest on airport parking call 510-633-2571.

San Jose International

Located just north of downtown San Jose, like Oakland Airport it is relatively easy to navigate and find parking in. Large and small air carriers fly to San Jose International.

For general information call 408-277-4759. For parking information call 408-293-6788.

CAR RENTAL

All the big rental outfits are represented in the Bay Area, most with numerous locations. Here are a few numbers to get you started.

- **Alamo,** 800-327-9633
- **Avis**, 800-831-2847
- **Budget**, 415-775-5800
- **Dollar**, 800-800-4000
- **Enterprise,** 415-441-3369 (downtown San Francisco) 415-697-9200 (San Francisco Int'l Airport)
- **Hertz**, 800-654-3131
- **Rent-A-Wreck**, 415-851-2627
- **Standard**, 800-953-CARS
- **Thrifty**, 800-367-2277

For a comprehensive look at Bay Area transit options look for the latest edition of the *San Francisco Bay Area Regional Transit Guide*. It's put out by the Metropolitan Transportation Commission and is available at many bookstores for about $4. If you have trouble locating it contact the MTC at 510-464-7700.

Taxis

San Francisco is served by a number of cab companies though city leaders would like to increase the number of licensed cabs on the street. Drivers, naturally, oppose such a move. Meanwhile, frustrated folks stand on street corners competing for taxis that may already be taken.

- **City Cab,** 415-468-7200
- **De Soto Cab,** 415-673-1414
- **Luxor Cab**, 415-282-4141
- **Veteran's Cab**, 415-552-1300
- **Yellow Cab**, 415-626-2345

IF YOU NEED an interim place to hang your hat, have no fear, there are a number of options in San Francisco. A note to the adventurous and/or budget minded newcomer: if you are considering one of the old-fashioned "residential hotels" that dot much of downtown San Francisco, keep in mind that these places typically offer just a small room with little more than a bed, dresser, chair and a desk. They are popular because they rent by the day, week or month, and because they are conveniently located near cheap eats and public transit. Unfortunately, these low-rent buildings are often located in the seedier parts of town, such as the southern half of Polk Street, the Fifth and Mission streets area south of Market Street, and the so-called "Tenderloin" which is just north of Market to the east and north of the recently opened New Main Library in the Civic Center. They are generally not for the faint of heart.

The following options are in area code 415. Low rates quoted are for one person per night; high rates quoted, for the most part, are for two persons per night. Of course, prices are subject to change (and may be negotiable).

INEXPENSIVE HOTELS

- **Canterbury Hotel**, 750 Sutter St., 474-6464, $80-100
- **Hotel Britton**, 112 7th St., 621-7001, $50-60
- **Royal Pacific Motor Inn**, 661 Broadway, 781-6661, $70-80

MEDIUM-PRICED HOTELS

- **Bedford Hotel**, 761 Post St., 673-6040, $90-110
- **Chancellor Hotel**, 433 Powell St., 362-2004, $100-120
- **Hotel Juliana**, 590 Bush St., 392-2540, $125-170
- **King George Hotel**, 334 Mason St., 781-5050, $115-125
- **The Raphael**, 386 Geary St., 986-2000, $100-140
- **York Hotel**, 940 Sutter St., 885-6800, $95-110

LUXURY HOTELS

- **The Clift**, 495 Geary St., 775-4700, $215-360
- **The Fairmont**, 950 Mason St., 772-5000, $135-245
- **The Grand Hyatt**, 345 Stockton St., 398-1234, $215-240
- **The Mark Hopkins**, 1 Nob Hill, 392-3434, $180-305
- **The Palace**, 2 New Montgomery St., 392-8600, $285-365

SHORT TERM APARTMENT RENTALS

A prime example of the high rise temporary apartment option is the Fox Plaza Apartment complex. Studios, one and two bedroom units are available in this 29-floor building, each with a panoramic view of San Francisco that may well be worth the high price. The building also has 24-hour security, a fitness center, underground parking and restaurants in the building. Cats are the only pets allowed, provided you pony up a $500 deposit.

- **Fox Plaza**, 1390 Market St., 800-863-3190; 415-626-6902

Studio	$795-920 per month
1 bedroom	$985-1235 per month
2 bedroom	$1305-2025 per month

HOSTELS/YMCA/YWCA

- **AYH Hostel Union Square**, 312 Mason St., 788-5604, $14-17
- **AYH Hostel Fort Mason**, Ft. Mason, Bldg., 240, 771-7277, $13-14
- **Globetrotters Inn**, 494 Broadway, 346-5786, $12-24
- **YMCA**, Administrative Office, 44 Montgomery St.,391-9622
- **YMCA Hotel**, 220 Golden Gate Ave., 885-0460, $28-38
- **YMCA Hotel**, 855 Sacramento St., 982-4412, $28-38

BED & BREAKFASTS

There are hundreds of B&Bs in the Bay Area, ranging in price from as low as $65 per night for a simple room in a private home to as much as $200 per night for an opulent unit in an historic Victorian or a self-contained carriage house or private cottage. **Bed and Breakfast International** has been providing information and reservations about local B&Bs since 1978 and boasts connections to more than 300 B&Bs and similar lodgings. Bed and Breakfast International is reachable at 415-696-1690, and on the World Wide Web at http://www.bbintl.com. The mailing address is P.O. Box 282910, San Francisco, CA 94128-2910.

HARDLY A DAY goes by when there's nothing to do or see in this culturally rich region. Many local events take place on an annual basis, making some of them seem like old friends. Here are just a few of the celebrations and remembrances you may want to experience for yourself.

January

- **Martin Luther King, Jr. Birthday Celebration**
  call for location, San Francisco, 415-771-6300

February

- **Black History Month Celebration**
  Westlake Park, Daly City, 415-991-8001
- **African-American History & Cultural Events**
  Oakland Museum of California, Oakland, 510-238-3401
- **Russian Festival**
  Richmond District, San Francisco, 415-921-7631

March

- **Chinese New Year's Golden Dragon Parade**
  Chinatown, San Francisco, 415-982-3000
- **St. Patrick's Day Parade**
  Market Street, San Francisco, 415-661-2700

April

- **Cherry Blossom Festival**
  Japantown, San Francisco, 415-563-2313
- **KQED Wine & Food Festival**
  Concourse Exhibition Center, San Francisco, 415-553-2200
- **San Francisco International Film Festival**
  call for theater locations, San Francisco, 415-992-5000

- **Berkeley Bay Festival**
  Berkeley Marina, Berkeley, 510-644-8623
- **Earth Day Celebration**
  Oakland Farmers' Market, Oakland, 510-452-3276
- **Youth Arts Festival**
  Berkeley Arts Center, Berkeley, 510-644-6893

May

- **Bay to Breakers foot-race**
  cross-city 7-mile run, walk and party, San Francisco
  415-808-5000 ext 2222
- **Carnaval**
  24th and Mission Streets, San Francisco, 415-826-1401
- **Cinco de Mayo Parade**
  24th and Mission Streets, San Francisco, 415-826-1401
- **Youth Arts Festival**
  M.H. de Young Museum, Golden Gate Park, San Francisco
  415-759-2916
- **Greek Festival**
  Greek Orthodox Cathedral, Oakland, 510-531-3400
- **Maritime Day**
  Jack London Square and Waterfront, Oakland, 510-814-6000

June

- **Haight Street Fair**
  Haight and Ashbury Streets, San Francisco, 415-661-8025
- **Lesbian, Gay, Bisexual & Transgender Celebration and Parade**
  numerous San Francisco locations, 415-864-3733
- **Stern Grove Midsummer Music Festival**
  Stern Grove, San Francisco, 415-252-6252
- **Union Street Festival**
  Union and Fillmore Streets, San Francisco, 415-346-4446
- **Festival at the Lake**
  Lake Merritt, Oakland, 510-286-1061

July

- **Comedy Celebration Day**
  Polo Field, Golden Gate Park, San Francisco
  415-777-8498 (sometimes held in August)
- **Fourth of July Celebrations**
  numerous San Francisco locations, 415-777-8498
- **Jewish Film Festival**
  UC Theatre, Berkeley
  Castro Theatre, San Francisco, 510-548-0556
- **KQED International Beer & Food Festival**
  Concourse Exhibition Center, San Francisco, 415-553-2200

- **Berkeley Kite Festival and West Coast Kite Flying Championships**
  Cesar Chavez Park, Berkeley Marina, Berkeley, 510-525-2755
- **Shakespeare in Oakland**
  Lakeside Park, Oakland, 415-666-2221

August

- **Berkeley Farmers' Market Cajun Festival**
  Martin Luther King, Jr. Park, Berkeley, 510-548-3333
- **Chinatown Street Fair**
  Chinatown, Oakland, 510-893-8979
- **San Francisco Shakespeare Festival**
  Golden Gate Park, San Francisco, 415-666-2221
- **Park Street Art and Wine Fair**
  Park Street, Alameda, 510-523-1392

September

- **A la Carte, a la Park**
  Sharon Meadow, Golden Gate Park, San Francisco, 415-383-9378
- **Opera in the Park**
  Sharon Meadow, Golden Gate Park, San Francisco, 415-861-4008
- **San Francisco Blues Fest**
  Ft. Mason, San Francisco, 415-826-6837
- **Italian Festival**
  Jack London Square, Oakland, 510-814-6000

October

- **Castro Street Fair**
  Castro Street, San Francisco, 415-467-3354
- **Columbus Day Parade**
  North Beach, San Francisco, 415-434-1492
- **Fleet Week**
  numerous locations, San Francisco, 415-705-5500
- **Great Halloween Art and Pumpkin Festival**
  Polk Street and Broadway, San Francisco, 415-346-4446

November

- **Christmas Tree Lighting**
  Ghirardelli Square, San Francisco, 415-775-5500
  Pier 39, San Francisco, 415-981-8030
- **Veteran's Day Parade**
  Market Street, San Francisco, 415-467-8218
- **Oakland Holidays Tree Lighting**
  Jack London Square, Oakland, 510-814-6000

December

- **Festival of Lights**
  Union Square, San Francisco, 415-922-0770
- **Sing-along *Messiah***
  Davies Symphony Hall, San Francisco, 415-431-5400
- ***Nutcracker***
  San Francisco Ballet, San Francisco, 415-861-1177

All numbers are area code 415 unless otherwise noted.

AIRPORTS

Oakland International Airport 510-577-4000
San Francisco International Airport .761-0800
San Jose International Airport 408-277-4759

AMBULANCE

All areas 911

ANIMALS

Animal bites 911
Animal Control 554-6364
Society for the Prevention of Cruelty to Animals 554-3000

BIRTH CERTIFICATES

SF County Health Department 554-2700

SF CITY/COUNTY GOVERNMENT

Assessor 554-5525
City Clerk 554-4267
City Hall 554-4000
District Attorney 553-1752
Health Department 554-2500
Marriage Licenses 554-4150
Mayor's Office 554-6141
Parking Commission 554-9800
Residential Parking Permits 554-5000
Public Utilities Commission 554-7316
Public Schools Office 241-6000
Rec and Parks 666-7200

Registrar of Voters 554-4375
Rent Board 554-9550
Supervisors 554-5184

CHILD ABUSE & NEGLECT

Domestic Violence Hotline 800-540-5433
SF Child Abuse Council 668-0494

CRISIS SERVICES

Alcoholics Anonymous 621-1326
American Red Cross 202-0600
Domestic Violence Hotline 800-540-5433
Gay Youth Talk Line 863-3636
Women Against Rape 647-7273

DENTAL SERVICES

Dental referral 800-DENTIST

EARTHQUAKE INFORMATION

California Seismic Safety Commission 916-322-4917
Earthquake Preparedness Program 510-540-2713

ELECTED OFFICIALS

SF Mayor 554-6141
California Governor 703-2218

FIRE EMERGENCY

All areas 911

HOUSING

State Fair Employment and Housing Department 800-884-1684
SF Rent Board 554-9550
SF Tenant's Union 282-5525

LIBRARIES

New Main 557-4400

MARRIAGE LICENSES

Information, San Francisco 554-4150

POLICE EMERGENCY

All areas 911

SPORTS

Golden State Warriors 510-639-7700
Oakland A's 510-638-0550
Oakland Raiders 510-639-7700
San Francisco 49ers 468-2249
San Francisco Giants 467-8000
San Francisco Spiders 656-3000
San Jose Clash 408-985-4625
San Jose Sharks 408-287-7070
Stanford University 723-1021
University of California, Berkeley 800-462-3277

TAXES

SF Tax Collector 554-4470
Internal Revenue Service 510-839-1040
State Franchise Tax Board 800-338-0505

TAXIS

City Cab 468-7200
De Soto Cab 673-1414
Luxor Cab 282-4141
Veteran's Cab 552-1300
Yellow Cab 626-2345
SuperShuttle 558-8500

TRANSPORTATION

Bay Area Rapid Transit (BART) 788-BART
MUNI 673-MUNI
AC Transit 800-559-4636
SamTrans 800-660-4287
CalTrain 800-660-4289
Golden Gate Transit 453-2100
CalTrans road information 557-3755

ZIP CODE INFORMATION

US Post Office 550-6500

A NATIVE OF Oxford, England, Michael Bower moved to California in 1967, and has been there ever since. He has lived in the San Francisco Bay Area for 20 years, in the city itself, as well as in the North Bay, on the Peninsula, and now in the East Bay. If it weren't for the trees in front of his house he'd be able to see the Golden Gate Bridge from his living room window. He's an award-winning broadcast journalist. There's nowhere else in the United States he'd rather live than the Bay Area. This is Michael's first book.

THE ORIGINAL, ALWAYS UPDATED, ABSOLUTELY INVALUABLE GUIDES FOR PEOPLE MOVING TO A CITY!

Find out about neigborhoods, apartment hunting, money matters, deposits/leases, getting settled, helpful services, shopping for the home, places of worship, belonging, sports/recreation, volunteering, green space, transportation, temporary lodgings and useful telephone numbers!

	#/COPIES		TOTAL
Newcomer's Handbook™ for Atlanta	_____	x $13.95	$_____
Newcomer's Handbook™ for Boston	_____	x $13.95	$_____
Newcomer's Handbook™ for Chicago	_____	x $12.95	$_____
Newcomer's Handbook™ for Los Angeles	_____	x $13.95	$_____
Newcomer's Handbook™ for Minneapolis/St. Paul	_____	x $14.95	$_____
Newcomer's Handbook™ for New York City	_____	x $16.95	$_____
Newcomer's Handbook™ for Washington, DC	_____	x $13.95	$_____
Newcomer's Handbook™ for San Francisco	_____	x $13.95	$_____

SUBTOTAL $_____

TAX (IL residents add 8.75% sales tax) $_____

POSTAGE & HANDLING ($4.00 first book, $.75 each add'l) $_____

TOTAL $_____

SHIP TO:

_____
Name

_____
Title

_____
Company

_____
Address

_____
City   State   Zip

_____
Phone Number

Send this order form and a check or money order
payable to: First Books, Inc.

First Books, Inc., Mail Order Department
P.O. Box 578147, Chicago, IL 60657
773-276-5911

Allow 2-3 weeks for delivery.

DO YOU THINK YOU KNOW SAN FRANCISCO BETTER THAN WE DO?
TELL US!

If you are the first to offer any new information about
San Francisco that is subsequently used in the next
Newcomer's Handbook™ for San Francisco,
we'll send you a free copy of our next edition.

SUGGESTIONS:

_____

_____

_____

_____

_____

YOUR NAME: _____

YOUR ADDRESS: _____

_____

_____

Help keep this guide current. If a listing has changed, let us know.

UPDATES:

_____

_____

_____

_____

Send to: First Books, Inc.
P.O. Box 578147, Chicago, IL 60657

Smart Business Travel

HOW TO STAY SAFE WHEN YOU'RE ON THE ROAD

Don't be scared, be prepared!

"Offers great safety tips for the business traveler." — *Chicago Tribune*

"Handy"— *Frequent Flyer*

"Contains plenty of common sense"— *Los Angeles Times*

"Recommended"— *Houston Chronicle*

	#/COPIES		TOTAL
Smart Business Travel	_____	× $12.95	$_____
TAX (IL residents add 8.75% sales tax)			$_____
POSTAGE & HANDLING ($3.00 first book, $.75 each add'l)			$_____
TOTAL			$_____

SHIP TO:

_____
Name

_____
Title

_____
Company

_____
Address

_____
City   State   Zip

_____
Phone Number

Send this order form and a check or money order
payable to First Books, Inc.

First Books, Inc. Mail Order Department
P.O. Box 578147, Chicago, IL 60657
773-276-5911

Allow 2-3 weeks for delivery.

FIRST BOOKS

Visit our web site at
http://www.firstbooks.com
for a sample of all our books.